𝔅𝔢𝔡𝔣𝔬𝔯𝔡𝔰𝔥𝔦𝔯𝔢'𝔰 𝔜

The Rural Scene

The
Book
Castle

Brenda Fraser-Newstead

First published November 1994
by
The Book Castle
12 Church Street
Dunstable
Bedfordshire LU5 4RU

ISBN 1 871199 47 6

Computer typeset by Keyword, Aldbury, Hertfordshire.
Printed in Great Britain by the Alden Press, Oxford.

The 'Bedfordshire's Yesteryears' oral history series is planned
to comprise:
volume 1 : The Family, Childhood and Schooldays
volume 2 : The Rural Scene
volume 3 : Craftsmen and Trades People
volume 4 : War Times and Civil Matters

Front Cover: The Hen-House, a familiar sight in pre-war times.
Herbert Stanton, Keysoe butcher and poultry rearer, photographed
in the late 1920s.
Photo: courtesy Mr A J Woodward.

CONTENTS

Page

FOREWORD 5
INTRODUCTION 7
ABOUT THE AUTHOR/ACKNOWLEDGEMENTS 8

VILLAGE LIFE 9
Introduction 11
Maulden Village 18
Village Changes 22
Village Growth 23
The Village Hall 23
The Women's Institute 24
The Village Shop 25
Village Services 27
The Village Officer 28
The Cottage 28
The Family Business 29
The Village Inn 30
The Inn-Keepers 31
The Hunt 32
Odd-Jobbing 34
The Conservationist 35
The Village Bachelor 36
Horse Dealing 37
Church and Chapel 37

THE BIG HOUSE 45
Introduction 47
The Big House at Wootton 50
The Family 50
The Staff 53
Good Times 54
Depressed Times 55
Village Folk Reminisce 58
The Big House at Sharnbrook 61

The Big House at Old Warden 64
The Squires 70
The Benefactors 73
Life in Service: Echoes from the Past 78
A Children's Nurse 78
A Chauffeur/Gardener 80
A Housemaid 82
The Cook's Daughter 85

THE FARM 91
Introduction 93
The Farmer 97
A Farmer's Daughter 104
The Farm House 108
The Cowman 109
The Horse Keeper 110
The Farm Worker 113
The Hedger and Ditcher 117
The Ploughboy 121
Working the Fields 122
The Bedfordshire Clanger 124
Thrashing 125
Moving Dung 128
Rabbiting 129

COUNTRY PLEASURES 131
Introduction 133
The Country Show 139
The Local 145
Day Trips and Other Pastimes 150
Single Days Spent in the Village 155
Single Days Spent in Bedford 156
Mayday Celebrations 157
The Statty 163

CONTRIBUTORS 167
INDEX TO LOCATIONS 183

FOREWORD

Rainbow School is one of fourteen Special Schools in Bedfordshire which, in all, serve a total of just over one thousand pupils. These schools provide for children with a wide range of needs, including moderate learning difficulties, physical disabilities, and emotional and behavioural problems – all needing particular and individual forms of support.

The pupils at Rainbow School tend to have profound and multiple learning difficulties and need some of the most intensive support of any pupils within Bedfordshire. Much of the equipment and many of the teaching aids required are not standard, and thus very expensive. Very high levels of teaching staff and care staff must also be maintained.

Mrs Fraser-Newstead's generous donation to the school of the proceeds of this book will be very welcome. Equally important, however, is the opportunity this gesture provides for publicising the valuable work being done at Rainbow School and the other Special Schools in Bedfordshire. Whilst reading about Village Life and Country Pleasures, I hope that readers will appreciate the important role these schools play in the lives of some of our more disadvantaged youngsters.

D G Wadsworth
Chief Education Officer,
Bedfordshire County Council

*The author
with David,
a remarkable
child.*

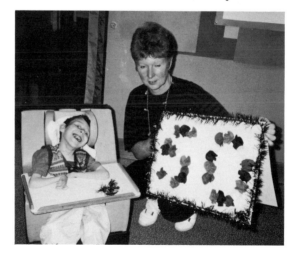

5

To Selena,
my very special child

INTRODUCTION

Continuing on from the popular Volume 1 of Bedfordshire's Yesteryears, entitled The Family, Childhood and Schooldays, published in 1993, this volume sets out to explore life as experienced by country folk in the early years of the twentieth century.

I was fortunate enough to be born in rural surroundings, and spent much of my youth walking the fields, collecting wild fruits, nuts and berries, mushrooming, bird-nesting, collecting wild flowers, and helping with harvesting and gleaning, potato and stone picking along with my mother and aunt. The delights of nature, its glorious seasonal array, delicate fragrances, joyous sounds, are forever memories of the countryside which I shall cherish in my heart. I hope in this volume to have conveyed something of my love of nature and of the countryside, and trust that the reader will gain pleasure from my insights.

In publishing my first volume I raised funds for research into Alzheimer's disease, an affliction mainly of the elderly. In publishing this second volume it is my intention to raise funds to benefit some very special young people whom I have known in recent years. The children of Rainbow School in Bromham taught me a great deal about the value of life itself, and enriched my life as I attempted to enhance theirs.

Brenda Fraser-Newstead

About the Author

Brenda Fraser-Newstead spent many years in the world of commerce and has been a teacher, author and examiner of Business Studies, and a company director. In recent years, however, she has forsaken that involvement and found rewarding work in social welfare and the teaching of children with special needs.

She originates from Wheathampstead in Hertfordshire, but her father was a Lutonian and she herself has lived in Bedfordshire for some twenty-five years.

Acknowledgements

The author wishes to thank, in particular, the contributors to this project, without whose help the book would not have materialised. Thanks also to the very many people, too numerous to mention personally, who have kindly given advice, assistance and support. A special word of thanks to the author's daughter, Yasmina, for her continued and valued assitance with editing and proof-reading.

Gratitude also to the following:

Mr D G Wadsworth,
    Chief Education Officer,
    Bedfordshire County Council
Mrs J Mason, Headteacher,
    Rainbow School, Bromham
Mr & Mrs G Donaldson,
    Bedford
The Bedfordshire Times
Mrs B Chambers,
    The Bedfordshire Magazine
The County Record Office
The Dunstable Gazette
Bedfordshire Social Services
Mr J Leech, Dunstable
Mrs H S Brown, Moggerhanger
Mr J Packer, Pertenhall
Mr E Sabey, Bedford

Mr E Baldock, Dunstable
Mr A Woodward, Keysoe
Mr M Jones, Sharnbrook,
    and Mr N Bowen
Mr W R Parrott,
    Milton Ernest (extracts
    from 'Sixty Years a
    Thatcher')
Mrs L Warner, Riseley
Mr E White, Ampthill
Mr N Bailey, Chief Executive,
    South Beds. Agricultural
    Society
Mr S Houfe & The White
    Crescent Press Ltd.
Staff at the Goldington Social
    Centre, Barkers Lane,
    Bedford

VILLAGE LIFE

A picturesque cluster of cottages, with typical 'timeless' quality, on The Green at Cardington.

Friends and neighbours in Radwell, still a close-knit and supportive village community in 1932.

VILLAGE LIFE

Introduction

The village community, one of our most enduring social institutions, is regarded with nostalgia by many townsfolk inspired by visions of a life of idyllic rural tranquility, amidst friendly neighbours, familiar faces, and the security which comes from being part of a community which cares. Idealized as this conception of rural life may be, the romanticist dreams of being awakened by the dulcet chirping of the dawn chorus of birds heralding a new day, the sweet sounds of church bells tolling, the vision of farm animals grazing in lush meadows, the merry clip-clop of horses in the lanes, the smells of newly-mown hay and grass from the garden and the aroma of a multitude of flowers of garden and wayside, the farmyard heavy with the scent of living creatures all permeating and stimulating the senses. The beauty and tranquility of the village green, its ponds, willows, ducks and wildlife, a focal point of local life and events – maypole dancing, feasts and fairs, bonfire night celebrations, memorials and remembrance services, and markets. The meandering stream flanked with reeds, stealthily picking its course through vales and skirting fields vibrant with the hues of lush crops, shades of brown, green, and yellow, dancing in the sun. Cottages huddled together clustered picturesquely, pastel tinted, thatched, tiled in hand-crafted delicacy, oak-beamed, lattice windows reflecting a little- changed environment, cradled unyielding against influences of change, enduring in character, beguiling in timeless qualities, at one with nature.

Village cottages: sympathetically adapted to serve the needs of present-day families, intent on preserving our rural heritage.

Snug beneath a golden thatch. Photo: courtesy Mrs Pack.

A Beautiful sturdy, oak timber-framed seventeenth century cottage with attractive infilled panels.

Decorative bargeboarding and traditional thatch beneath an ornamental, spiralling chimney in hand-crafted Bedfordshire Yellows. Photo: courtesy Mr & Mrs Gosland

Examples abound in this county of typical village architecture – the snug thatch, stone walls, rough-cast, pebble dashed and colour-washed, decorative pargeting, clay roof tiles of fish scale and pantiles, slate roofs, tile-hung walls, bargeboard gables, dormers, varieties of chimneys, flint and brickwork, diaper brickwork, herringbone infill of timber beams. A wealth of design, a joy to behold: evidence of the skill of centuries of craftsmen.

Many a cottage garden still contains colourful and herbaceous borders, flanking lawns and pathways, scented shrubs and a traditional array of flowers – lavender, rose, honeysuckle, hollyhocks, chrysanthemums, lilac, daffodils, lilies of the valley, paeony, pansy, sweet pea and golden rod. A statute of 1589 in the time of Elizabeth I declared that no rural cottages were to be constructed or buildings converted for habitation unless each contained an area of four acres. Thus, the cottage garden, or smallholding, could support

Former bakery. Enchanting old clay-tiled roof and red-brick walls, weathered, time-textured, tinged ochre, brown, beige, exuding warmth and character, garden ablaze with colour.
Photo: courtesy Mrs S J M Akerman

Beauty in simplicity: pastel-tinted rendering, plain-tiled roof with ridge-tiles, dormers and lattice windows. A typical estate cottage, complete with well. Photo: courtesy Mr J Mayor.

livestock and limited crop, fruit and vegetable growth. Little wonder the villages were self-sufficient! Few cottages now have large gardens and those that did, until recently, have fallen foul of developers bent on in-filling.

Idealized as this portrait of the village may be, Bedfordshire contains many lovely villages, created by man and nature, each having its own appeal, and each dear to those whose lives have been shaped and enriched by the village experience.

The reality of the village to some degree matches this common perception and, in Bedfordshire villages and elsewhere, the majority of village-dwellers are concerned to preserve the unique aspects of a traditional way of life. There are features of village life which have endured through centuries and these are associated with the seasonal changes which nature has evolved, and with our Christian beliefs and the celebrations associated with them.

The church remains the focal point of the village: a place for worship, weddings, christenings and funerals, and a meeting place. Religious festivals – Christmas, with candle-lit carol services; Easter, concluding a period of Lent and for some, self-denial; Harvest Festivals to celebrate and give thanks for the successful conclusion of months of work on the land (even though now mechanised) and the bounties of nature yielded up for the benefit of all. The traditional skills of campanology – bell ringing – have survived and the sound of the bells on a quiet summer's evening is a joy to savour.

Our churches and churchyards are monuments to the generations preceding us. They are symbols of pride and lovingly tended by those fortunate to have associations with them. Many village dwellers have relatives buried in the churchyards which are themselves carefully tended, with closely mown grass and fresh flowers. The yews, standing proudly erect, as sentinels, often pre-date the church itself, and add to the timeless serenity of the place.

The Ridgemont Brass Band. Many village communities took pride in their brass band, which would play at local events and on special occasions. Photo: courtesy Mr Chris Creamer.

The Men's Bible Class, 'an invaluable institution in the life of the Methodist Church in Dunstable, and in the wider life of the town and district'. Photo: courtesy The Dunstable Gazette.

Over the years the church has organised activities and outings, and fostered Christian fellowship through Sunday School and societies such as The Girls' Friendly Society, The Band of Hope, The Bible Class, The Choir and the Girls' Brigade. Mothers' Meetings, Youth Clubs and Creches. Many elderly church patrons were and still are, accommodated in almshouses provided by the church. In villages and towns, the church has welded the community.

The Sabbath may not now be so rigorously observed as a day of rest as it was in times of greater religious fervour, but there are those who rise to the call of the bells on a Sunday morning and wend their way to prayer, and for those of a lesser religious persuasion, Sunday may be spent enjoying a social drink in the 'local' and after a lunch, taking a bracing stroll or passing the day pottering about in the garden. For most, Sunday is still a day of relaxation.

The office of Church Warden was established over eight hundred years ago, and responsibilities in earlier times were for the maintenance of the church fabric, accounting for income from church properties and land, organising relief for the parish poor, dealing with parish taxes and so on. This is now an honorary post of officer assisting the vicar, since in 1921 parish councils assumed financial responsibilities.

Most villages are characterised by their relative isolation and self-sufficiency, most containing certain elements which make up a village: the manor house, church, shop, school, inn (the main social centre, place for exchange of gossip, often the location of the colourful Hunt meet), village hall, the village green, and outlying farms. In earlier times one would expect to find a bakery, brewery, blacksmith's workshop, carpenter and undertaker's workshop, the cobbler, the miller. Travelling salesmen delivered to villages and many requirements were brought to the door including fresh meat, vegetables, milk, and items of clothing: the tallyman almost bonded to the community he served, the many with limited financial resources.

No longer a community of those employed on the land, of farm workers, shop keepers, tradesmen, craftsmen, servants and so on, the villages survive and benefit by the mobility and affluence which commuters now bring to bear. The fabric of the village is being preserved and its traditions upheld. If development can be checked, the social cohesion which the village community fosters, may also be preserved.

Breathtakingly beautiful, a reed-thatched cottage with decorative ornamental ridges. A wealth of beams, and immense character. Well-tended gardens overlook the village green.
Photo: courtesy Mrs E M Mayhan.

Maulden Village

Maulden is situated in a particularly fertile area well known for its market gardening of vegetable and salad crops. Part of this land was sold by the Duke of Bedford as smallholdings during the depression and this has encouraged private enterprise and led to a flourishing trade for local and London markets over the years.

'There were snipe to be seen along the banks of the brook, but that is many years ago. Pied wagtails were also to be seen in fair numbers and could be seen bathing in the big puddles in

Helping in the fields at Maulden. Haymaking, a pleasurable and useful activity and another opportunity for social interaction and enjoyment of the outdoors. Photo: courtesy Mrs Peacock.

the "Knoll" before it was tidied up. I agree that it now looks much more attractive with the well-kept grass and flowers but I miss the little black and white birds with their jerky movements. We still have lots of starlings and sparrows and in my small garden I have robins, thrushes and blackbirds. I once heard the sparrows referred to by a local lad, as hedgey-bets. We now hear the calling of collar-doves – kuk-coo-coo. I believe they have only appeared in comparatively recent times. Last year there was a brilliantly coloured woodpecker on a nut tree in "Knoll Lane", but I have not seen it for some time now.

I saw one grey squirrel run along the top of my fence recently – but no more. One year when my small garden ran wild and I had a magnificent display of thistles I had gold-finches and green-finches visiting. Bull-finches also come and are very pretty if not always welcome where there are fruit buds.

Nightingales used to sing in Kimbersey Lane (as well as Berkley Square)! There were skylarks trilling away above the allotments as I worked up there in the early days of the war. It was interesting to watch their ascent towards the sky in an almost vertical line. That was before the advent of tractors when the allotments were hand-dug and surroundings were much more peaceful.

Hedgehogs were frequent visitors. On one occasion a local lad who was something of a nature lover brought a sack containing five baby hedgehogs to school. He tipped them out on the doormat and we had a real live nature lesson.

We used to go by way of Church Path, through the churchyard and into the fields to the pond. Church Path at that time had banks on either side and growing on the banks were many harebells – dainty blue flowers. The children called them "Fairy thimbles". Along with the harebells there grew a lot of yarrow. Yarrow tea was a well known and accepted remedy for coughs and colds. An old gentleman asked me to make some yarrow tea for him which I did, according to his instructions. But I don't think it could have been successful as I was never asked to make any more!

There were many grasshoppers on the banks too. Queer creatures to watch.

By the pond in the fields we used to see many beautiful dragon flies. In among the grass of the fields there were many different fungi – some brightly coloured.

Horses grazed in the fields. One day on passing through, one of them rested his head on my shoulder and escorted us to the exit from the fields, much to the delight of my grandson, who was about four at the time.

Knoll Lane was once flanked by a three-foot high hedge of mixed holly, hawthorn and nut stubs on the right, kept cut down to that height while the adjoining ground was cultivated with beans, lettuce, carrots and the famous Maulden celery. The "hedge" is now twenty feet high. Standing on that ground was an old-fashioned copper (a which Mr James Stanford used for cooking food for his pigs when he lived in the cottage which used to be No. 18. His pigs were kept at the back of numbers 14, 16 and 18, and the tenants of the three cottages shared the ground which is now lawns and gravel drive.

There was a roadway down from No. 18 to the lane wide enough for a horse and cart to pass through. A stable stood at the junction with "Knoll Lane" and this housed Mr Charles Stanford's horse. Charles Stanford was the son of James Stanford. The roadway has become a rose-garden, and where the stable stood there has this year (1987) been a lush display of Japonica – some red and some yellow of the same family. We used to call the yellow "Bachelors buttons" in my youth. No need in that spot for artificial fertiliser. Laburnum has also bloomed luxuriantly in that corner. There was a well opposite No. 18 which was in constant use providing a water supply for numbers 14, 16 and 18.

On the left-hand side of the lane, almost opposite the roadway, stood a small cottage which we always called "The dolls' house". It was just like a small child's first drawing of a house – two windows at the top and two below with the front door in the middle – no back door. Quite a large family was brought up there. There was a shed built on to one side where all the cooking and washing for the household was done. Those were the days when wash-day was always Monday, and the housewife was judged by the whiteness of her clothes on the washing line and how early she got them out to dry. She was lucky if she had an old-fashioned wringer or mangle with wooden rollers.

Just inside what is now the entrance to No. 20 stood one of the real old-fashioned greengage trees and opposite what is now the front door of No. 20 was what the local folks call a "hovel". This was a new word to me when I came to Maulden. It was used to describe and open-fronted shed. In this "hovel" Mr George Taylor kept the cart in which he carried market garden produce to Bedford and Luton.

A nineteenth century Maulden agricultural worker, proud of his calling – 'his own boss on his own ground'. Photo: courtesy Mrs Peacock.

A turn to the left at the top of the lane led past two cottages which had originally been the "work-house" for Maulden. They have now been restored to form one house. I remember seeing a tree laden with peaches in the garden of one of them in what seemed a perfect summer.

Further along, on the same side, stood the old blacksmith's shop. This was demolished by a runaway tank in the early days of the 1939–1945 war. The ground on which it stood has been used as a builder's yard but at present lies waste.'

GLADYS WALLIS

Village Changes

'I have seen many changes in Wootton over the years, many for the better. There were no WCs for many years, just buckets. All around Wootton these were used and emptied in the garden. There was no sewage collection, and everyone buried their own! There was no electric, but just candles or paraffin lamps. Fires and ovens were combined and the cooking was done on the range. Cooking was sometimes done over the fire. Despite this, there were no house fires as I recall.

I think it's sad that much of original Wootton village is vanishing and that housing developments will spoil the village. There is now talk of demolishing the old Wootton Primary School, built for the village children in 1877 by Sir Phillip Payne.'

FREDERICK BURRAWAY

Village Growth

'When I married, we lived in our family home, the house in which my mother had been born, and where I still live (in Thurleigh). The village has changed enormously, however. Before the war there were only about two houses built, then the Council built about six or eight properties in the 1930s, in the High Street. After the war there was extensive building, including a block of flats right in the middle of our lovely country village – much to my disgust. It is a dormer village now and not many of the old original people are left, but it is a good community. The villagers held a New Year's party at the village hall this year and this was very good. A concert party came from Luton, the bar was open late and we had quite a happy day.'

JOHN 'JACK' THORNE

The Village Hall

'My wife and I moved to Pertenhall in 1947. The parson was in charge of the village hall at that time: it had been derelict when he took it over. It was built for £400 in 1907, a donation from the village benefactors, the Martin family. When we moved into the village the church commissioners wanted to sell it off, but we borrowed money from local farmers to get the roof done and continued fundraising to restore it. Mr Litchfield, a local carpenter, loaned the tools for village people to put a new floor in. We had toilets installed, a kitchen, and a false ceiling. It was an asset to the village and local people. We had whist drives which were run by the Conservative Party, the Men's Club, and a play group three days a week. The Women's Institute used it and it was rented for private parties. I have a watch engraved "To John from a Grateful Village", which was a gift to me for all the work I did on the village hall over many years.'

JOHN PACKER

The Women's Institute

The WI has been described as Britain's foremost women's movement and branches are active in both towns and villages throughout the county, as indeed they are throughout the country.

The WIs began in 1915 and were established for the purpose of improving the quality of life for country women everywhere. The depression, the war, and the population drift from the countryside, all contributed to a concern to preserve and regenerate country life and traditional values, to inform and educate the women who played their part in supporting rural communities. This awareness of the important contribution of women within the community, coincided with the emergence of the suffragette movement and the opportunities for women to enter industry and contribute to the war effort. Many founder members were leaders of their day, fighters for the cause of women, revolutionaries and women of vision. The WIs consisted of women of all classes, but although democratic, the President was often a prominent member of the community, such as the Lady of the Manor – probably because these were the women with the confidence to execute the task and provide leadership. One advantage was that often these women were well connected, and could bring influence to bear at local and central government levels, through their spouses – if not in their own right.

It was intended that the WI movement would create a renewed interest in village life and that the welfare of home life would be advanced. Farming, the rural communities and the provision of home-grown foods, were vital, in order to support the war effort. The WIs were formed under the auspices of the Agricultural Organisation Society (largely funded by the Board of Agriculture) in order to 'start local societies of farmers, smallholders and growers so that they may co-operate together to buy what they needed, sell what they grew, and in any other ways, to the benefit of agriculture'. The object of the movement included such things as the study of home economics, provision of a centre for education and social intercourse and for all local activities, to encourage home and local industries, develop co-operative enterprises and to stimulate interest in the agricultural industry. The WIs later became independent of their government-backed sponsorship, when in 1917 the National Federation was formed and the WIs became self-governing.

Among the first activities undertaken by the WIs were talks on cookery, household affairs and gardening, baking, jam-making and flower and vegetable growing to sell for profit. Market stalls were a regular feature, providing outlets for goods produced. Food production and fund-raising in support of troops, were important functions of the WIs in the early years, and it could be said that the war was a catalyst to the development of the movement.

The WIs have continued to work at raising awareness of issues important in particular, to rural communities, and at improving conditions in rural communities. Present-day concern has focussed on preservation of the countryside, education, health and social issues. Meetings provide an opportunity for social interaction, mutual understanding, and cohesion within the new communities which are emerging in our villages. Membership informs, provides a challenge and opportunities for self-development, and lends support for local causes of importance. The WIs have helped to preserve traditions of the countryside, and rural crafts, and have focused attention on rural life and the village community. Their latest contribution in this county is the publication 'Bedfordshire Within Living Memory' which contains personal accounts of life in Bedfordshire during the first half of the twentieth century.

The Village Shop

The most marked difference between present-day shops and the shops of the past is the impersonal service modern shops offer, and the fact that most shops are now purpose-built and fitted whereas shops in the past were usually the front parlour of the family home. This was the traditional family business, with the family occupying rooms to the rear, and bedrooms above the shop. As a customer entered, the bell would jingle, and summons the shopkeeper from his or her private part of the house, to greet the customer over the wooden counter.

Village shops tended to stock all manner of things, being 'general stores', and anything a customer wanted, which was not available, would be obtained in time for the next visit. The village shop usually incorporated the Post Office, which also attracted regular business. Sweets, tobacco, habadashery, hardware, groceries!

Another distinctive feature of the village shop was the aroma which emanated from a range of goods, many of which were unwrapped. Sacks containing all manner of things from sugar, to dried fruits, all waiting to be weighed and wrapped. Cooked hams and meats, sliced and weighed to order. Candles, paraffin, carbolic soap, herbs, black-lead polish for the grate, Brasso to polish the brass – an investment in olden times, as spare money invested in brass could be easily converted to cash in times of need, hence the term 'brass' being a slang expression for 'money'. A vast range of cigarettes, and tobacco, firelighters and bundles of firewood. Biscuits in tins or jars. Blue Bags for washing whites or for use on wasp stings and insect bites, rows of sweets in glass jars, Sherbert Dabs, loose Sherbert, Sweet cigarettes, Candy Mice, Licorice, Pontefract Cakes, Dolly Mixtures, Black Jacks, Aniseed Balls, Gob Stoppers. Such variety for a penny or two, tantalising for children bewildered by the choice.

No such thing as 'self-service' in these shops. Friendly gossip while waiting to be served, or a friendly chat with the shop-keeper while your order was searched out, weighed and priced. A more relaxed, sociable activity than rushing around a huge hanger of a store, snatching pre-packed and bar-coded standard items off shelves before queueing in silence, robot-like at the check-out.

Most village shops contained polished wooden chairs for the customers' convenience and villagers would enjoy the opportunity the experience offered for conversing, and keeping up-to-date with happenings in the village. News spreads fast in small communities, and local news was of much more importance to most people than national or international news. A social centre, the village shop. Open all hours? Not so, as shops opened in normal working hours and this meant closing at 5.00pm or 5.30pm – no opening to 9.00pm or 10.00pm seven days a week. However, if something were needed which couldn't wait for opening time, a customer could always knock on the back door and would be led through into the shop and served without fuss or embarrassment. Payment in cash, or groceries and goods could be listed in an order book (a simple note-book), totted up and paid for at the end of the week. For the elderly, an order book would be dropped off at the shop and the shop-keeper would arrange for a delivery boy to cycle round with a box containing the order. Personal delivery for no extra charge, and another opportunity for social interaction.

Village Services

'The village blacksmith used to trade on the Fields Road site, which is now occupied by Wootton Garage, and this was a favourite meeting place for people in the village, being warm and inviting inside, and being situated across the road from the pub! The blacksmith was always in demand, making horseshoes and shoeing the many local horses, the majority of which were working horses, of course.

The village tailor was Mr Sinfield, who lived and traded in the house on the corner opposite the present Post Office, known locally as Luniss's Corner, as it had once been the home of Robert Edward Luniss, a local benefactor, from whose bequest of property in the village to the Wootton charities, various local people have benefitted.'

CONSTANCE ROBINSON

The Village Officer

'I was Clerk to the Parish Council [Thurleigh] for about thirty years, Secretary to the Village Hall Committee since its inception in 1929, Secretary to the Flower Show held every August Bank Holiday Monday for many years, Trustee of the local Jeffries and Harveys Charity, Secretary of the Baptist Church, Life President of the Bedfordshire Baptist Association, one time member of the Baptist Union Council representing Bedfordshire, and Treasurer of the Cricket Club.

During the war I helped with fund-raising for the Forces, Red Cross and other. I worked on the farm during the first world war, and maintained hostels and farm buildings for the War Agricultural Committee in the second world war. There were hostels at Bolnhurst, Ravensden and Milton Ernest – used by Land Army girls.'

FREDERICK WILDMAN

The Cottage

'Water had to be obtained from a single tap situated about twenty-five yards from the rear of each block of cottages. One washed oneself and the dishes in a bowl placed on a table in a kitchen cum living room and a bath was taken in a hip-bath placed in front of the fireplace. Clothes were washed in a communal wash-house some distance from the back door. The lavatories were in line with the wash-house and had never heard the word "flush". Some cottages had two rooms down and two up, others had only one down, one up and a small box room. This provided very poor accommodation since it should be remembered that most of the families in those days had about seven or more children. Lighting was by candles or oil lamps. The one good point about these tenancies was the fact that they had a very long garden which the people cultivated in order to improve their general standard of living. Each family would keep a number of chickens and ducks and the men would go out and shoot a couple of rabbits as and when required. Nothing was wasted, the meat was *eaten, the feathers were used to fill pillow-cases and the rabbit skins were cured then secured to the steps of the stairs or made into a bedside rug. Wood was the main source of fuel. It was the practice to buy a "side of bacon" which was then cured with brine and hung up in the kitchen after which pieces were cut off for the various meals. (I was informed that there was an abattoir behind what is now the delightful thatched cottage, 5 St. John's Road, Moggerhanger, from where it was possible to purchase various parts of a pig at different times of the year.) In each cottage there was always a quantity of onions and shallots plaited and hung from the ceiling. These were used in stews, roasted or eaten raw. It was possible to go to the farm and buy "skimmed milk" for very little cash and this was generally poured over boiled potatoes to make a very satisfying meal. Wine was made from potatoes or various plants picked by the children who would also spend many happy hours picking blackberries which were then made into jam. Another type of jam was made from vegetable marrows. Fruit was bottled and the jars were sealed with paraffin-wax (candle fat) boiled in an old saucepan. A type of "freezer" was then made by digging a hole in the garden, placing the jars into it and then covering them over with soil. Father would dig out a jar whenever fruit was on the menu.'*

H S BROWN

The Family Business

'There was a bakery in Bedford Road, and the village baker for many years was Mr Keep of Hall End. The Juff family who now own Wootton Riding School, were also family bakers, supplying Wootton with bread, and providing a baking service for weekend roasts, cakes, and especially Christmas cakes.

The present owner of Wootton Riding School is Mr Bill Juff, and it was his father and grandfather who established and ran the bakery. There was no riding stable at that time, but Mr Juff's father had a horse and trap and I believe this is the same trap which "young Bill" now uses for local weddings. Bill Juff was born at the family home and bakery in Hall End Road, and was raised by his parents and grandfather, who shared the same address. I was a pupil at the village school which stood next to the Cock Inn in Bedford Road, and I still recall vividly, Bill's first day at school. He became very excited on hearing a passing horse and trap, which he recognised as his grandfather's, and since the windows were high and he couldn't see out of them, he pleaded with the teacher to be allowed out of school to see his grandad. Theirs was a close-knit family, and being animal lovers, they nurtured in Bill a love of animals, particularly horses, which have been a passion throughout his lifetime. A close friend of this family was Raymond Burraway, a Wootton man and ex. Grenadier Guard, who has worked at the stables as Groom for many years, and whose father worked at the Juff's bakery all his life, making and delivering bread in and around the village.'

CONSTANCE ROBINSON

The Village Inn

The village pub of the past was not the smart up-market place many of us know today, and look forward to visiting on special occasions – birthday lunches, Mother's Day lunches, Christmas dinners or a special outing for drinks and a meal when the mood takes us. We all scan the local papers and read pub advertisements: which one shall we try? Perhaps a nice drive to wherever, a drink and lunch. Pubs with atmosphere, warm pubs, pubs which serve good meals, pubs which have our favourite brew of beer or lager. We can pick and choose now that we're all mobile, and the children can come provided we all eat.

What a far cry from the pub of the past, which catered for local trade and from which children were excluded by law and wives and women were excluded by custom! The village pub was the social centre of the village and a place for working men to relax and discuss work, or gardening, the allotment, local goings-on. Old village 'boys' would take their dogs for a stroll to the 'local', and the dogs would sit harmless on the flagstones, patiently awaiting the walk home. The fire crackling, the clock ticking, otherwise silence. No fruit machines bleeping, no music, no wall-to-wall carpeting with dogs strictly forbidden!

For hard-working men – and most work involved physical labour – the pub offered a chance to relax and unwind, and villagers would talk over their pint and over a game of shove-ha'penny, skittles, dominoes, crib or a number of card games. An institution, the pub, frequented by locals, all friends and neighbours, a personal experience and a reaffirmation of the bonds which existed among members of small village communities.

'The Stagsden pubs catered for local trade. Most people had their local pub where they met their friends. After work there was tea, then the allotment to work, then the pub for a pint and home for supper and bed. Most people started work at 6am each day, getting the horses ready, and harnessed.

My dad's pub night was a Saturday. The Friendly Society was started to provide money in sickness or death, for burial expenses. They used to meet in the Club Room at the pub once a month. This was another night out. Women didn't go to the pub, whilst they were young at any rate.' HORACE WELCH

Arthur Thompson, Landlord of the Flower Pot Public House in Tavistock Street, Bedford.

The Inn-Keepers

'My uncle, – my mother's brother – kept a pub called Wait for the Waggon, near Greenhill Street [in Bedford]: it is still there now. Another uncle, Arthur, was landlord of the Flower Pot Public House in

Tavistock Street, Bedford. This was when I was about twelve or fourteen. I remember the area well. There was a little pub at the corner of Harpur Street and a cake shop and cafe called Manns. The boys from the old Bedford Modern School would come dashing across the road in the break, for buns, ice-cream cornets and so on. This was known as 'The Bun Shop.'

EDITH 'IRENE' CORNWELL

'My maternal grandmother was one-time landlady of the Goat Public House in Bedford, and she also owned several cottages in Allhallows Lane. These she sold after re-marrying (now Mrs Page) and these were eventually demolished and the present Job Centre erected on the site. My father's brother, Uncle Harry Lawson, was landlord of the Golden Lion, probably in the 1920s. His son, Jack Lawson, was landlord of the Black Diamond Public House on the site of the present County Hall. Cousin Beatrice Lawson, Uncle Harry's daughter, kept the Fox and Hounds Public House at Clapham. The Spirits Licence for this house was transferred from the White Horse at Stagsden when my future in-laws closed that house down to become a private dwelling. My brother Bert was Landlord of the Sun Inn at Felmersham.'

IVY FLUTE

The Hunt

'One interest of mine over the years has been hunting. I was a member of the Oakley Hunt for about fifty years. I last rode with them on my eightieth birthday, when the horse fell! I've had a lot of practice at falling off. The Oakley Hunt was formed in the 19th century in Oakley, when the village was largely owned by the Duke of Bedford. The Hunt moved to Milton Ernest a hundred and fifty years ago to new kennels, at a time when there were two packs of hounds (dogs and bitches) and thirty horses. It later moved to Melchbourne. Before the war the Hunt met four days a week but this has now been reduced to two days. Much is changing now, including

The Fox and Hounds Public House at Clapham. One-time landlady, Beatrice Lawson.

The Sun Inn, Felmersham. One-time landlord, Bert Lawson.

attitudes to the sport, and the countryside itself, with housing developments and urbanisation. The Hunt has a tradition of well-attended social functions such as cocktail parties and the Hunt Ball, which used to be held at Melchbourne but is currently held at Woburn'.

JOHN CAMPION

The Oakley Hounds at Milton Ernest.

Odd-Jobbing

'In the winter months my father would leave the thatching and do any other jobs that came along such as tree felling, soot sowing, hedge layering, digging, corn setting with dibs, threshing corn with machines and flail, ditching, grave digging, etc. I well remember helping my father to set a field of horse beans for a farmer with a dib and line. It was on February 14th, St. Valentine's Day, when we started to set the beans and when they began to grow, the straight rows down

the field were a joy to behold. An old saying in those days was "to put four beans in the hole, one for the pigeon, one for the crow, one to rot and one to grow".

These and other jobs would see us through the cold winter months and then when the warmer weather arrived we would return to thatching again.

WALTER 'REG' PARROTT

Sid Summerlin, farm worker, odd-jobbing in retirement.

The Conservationist

'About our home [in Renhold], my personal views are that I don't want it developed, not in my lifetime. As a matter of fact I have turned down some good offers, and they won't get it, I'll sit on it as long as I am alive because I feel that the environment has been so taken over with concrete and somebody has to save it and stop this wanton destruction of the land, which I feel the country can ill-afford. I believe I am a realist. My home is a very old property, the bricks were

made in the village by hand, years ago, but they are very tough and well-made. When the decorative chimneys needed repairs I found a craftsman to do it and he made a beautiful job of it. There are six of these houses, the old estate cottages – the Howbury Estate. Each one had a small plot of land and they were like smallholdings then. Most of the village was sold off around 1923, at the time of the agricultural depression. Much of the land in the area belonged to the Polhills and the Page-Turners, who were related. They were, and still are, large landowners. They have land in London and many other places. Some members of this family were missionaries overseas, in China and other countries.

A lot of people would like my land for housebuilding, but I won't let it go. There is so much wild life on that ground that whilst I am alive it will not be used for anything else. I know there are deer, I can hear them calling when I am in bed at night. They are very partial to my tulips you know.'

WILLIAM CONSTANT

Village Bachelor

Sid Summerlin, farm-worker, lived with his mother [in Stagsden] until she died, and then with his sister until she died. His bungalow overlooks fields and woods to the rear. Pictures of harvest scenes adorn the walls of his living-room, and china shire horses are given pride of place on his display unit.

Sid has only had the doctor once in his whole life, which was 'recently', when he fractured his wrist hedging and was off work for three months. During this time he was paid from the Sick Club, the National United Order of Tree Gardeners Friendly Society. He has been in good health all his life (he says with more than a slight wheeze), and has smoked all his life – an 'occasional smoker'. He confesses that he smoked old man's beard, the stem of it, when he was at school. He has become well-established at his local pub, the Royal George in Stagsden, where his picture bears testimony to his presence, and where his seat at the bar is permanently reserved.

Asked about women in his life, Sid replies with a distinctly boyish charm, 'what do I want with women?'. He is reputed to be the shy village bachelor!

Horse Dealing

'Another interesting feature of life in the village was when between fifty and one hundred horses of all types, from the heavy cart horses, hunters, cobs and ponies to the brood mares with their dainty foals would come into the village en route *to a horse fair in a distant village or town. To keep these horses herded together two or three men would be riding on horseback whilst the owner and dealer named "Woolley" would be at the rear, sitting in a buggy drawn by a pony. A halt would be called outside the Queen's Head [Milton Ernest] and probably a deal would take place with one or two of the local farmers for an odd horse or two. As part of the inspection of the horse, one of the men would run it up and down the road for the farmer to see its actions. He would also inspect the legbone to make sure that no ring bones were present. Another point to watch was the age of the animal, to check which the teeth were inspected, this being one way of telling the age of a horse.'*

WALTER 'REG' PARROTT

Church and Chapel

'My family have always been active church members. My grandfather was an organist and father too, both of them self-taught. One vicar by the name of Wiggins, looked after two parishes then, Souldrop and Knotting. Most of the village people were churchgoers and at harvest festival and the Knotting Feast the church was packed out. In summer we used to walk across the fields to church and in winter we went to chapel: this chapel has since been made into a house. People who attended both church and chapel were known as "Devil Dodgers"!

Years ago women didn't go into church without covering their heads – women and girls. Straw hats were worn in summer and felt in winter.

Wives were good managers then – they always made their own clothes. We had a bath once a week, whether we needed it or not, and underclothes were changed once a week. Everything had to be clean on Sunday morning, ready for church. You couldn't do washing or gardening on a Sunday, it really would have been frowned upon. Dirty washing was put aside until Monday and most women had Monday for wash day.'

WINIFRED ALLAN

'I went through the Junior Sunday School to the Senior School, reaching the top class when I was round about fourteen years of age. There were some twenty of us. This would be in the year 1884. We were just about the age when boys think they are too big for the Sunday School. At this time I became an apprentice in the tailoring department of Mr Charles Lockhart, who was then our Sunday School Superintendent. He was keenly interested in us and a meeting was held at his house to consider what steps could be taken to form another and more suitable class for us. Mrs B. George, the wife of Superintendent George, who lived at the Police Station, Icknield Street [Dunstable], a school teacher, took a keen interest in us and often invited us to her home to tea, giving us many quiet and appealing talks on the Love of God. Mrs Bennett also, who lived at Moreton House, West Street, became greatly interested in our welfare. A Class was eventually established which was called "The Select Bible Class", afterwards becoming "Young Men's Bible Class", Mrs George and Mrs Bennett acting as Joint Leaders.

W H HUTCHINS and THE JOURNAL

The Men's Bible Class Orchestra in 1910. Printed by Parsons of Dunstable and used to publicise the Jubilee of the Men's Bible Class 1886–1936. Photo: courtesy Mr E Baldock.

'Bell ringing was another thing I used to do in my young days, in fact I was a bell ringer for thirty years in Wootton. There were six of us and we rang the bells every Sunday, at Christmas time and New Year's Eve. We rang the New Year in and then rang for Christmas morning at 7 o'clcock. I used to go up with the older men when I was about nine or ten, and I had number four – picked it up.

Every time anyone died the bells were rung, of course, and when they were buried. The gravedigger pulled the bell down but couldn't pull it up. Being young, I had the strength to pull it up for him. We ringers were paid a funeral toll of two shillings. The squire and the vicar used to come and pay us when the funeral was over. The squire was Sir Phillip Payne, and he came to church every Sunday. He was a short fellow, used to enter by the back door and sat in the rectory. His daughter, Mrs Doyne Ditmus, died at the age of ninety and I *saw her laid to rest. She was buried in the family vault in the churchyard, near the vestry door, and she was the last of the family to be buried there.'*

FREDERICK BURRAWAY

'We always went to Sunday School and church in our family, in fact we normally went three times on Sundays. It was a special treat when we visited Elstow Church. There used to be prizes for full attendance at Sunday School and for learning the scriptures. I still have my last prize, which was a Bible.'

HILDA HAYDEN

'The church was the centre of social life for the young people of our village years ago. I belonged to the Girls' Friendly Society, known as GFS, and I was also in the choir and went to choir practice one evening each week. I was a member of the Band of Hope at the Wesleyan Chapel, where I had to swear to be a teetotaller! We were occasionally given magic lantern shows, which were quite a treat and attracted a good audience. Each Sunday there was Sunday School and then the church service. I became a Sunday School teacher myself when I was fourteen.'

SARAH HILLS

'I was a member of the Baptist Church for many years, and was baptised there in 1926. I was a Sunday School teacher and church deacon. When I was a young man about fifteen or seventeen, I was friendly with a fellow whose father and grandfather were bell ringers. We two boys were learning bell ringing. Parents saw to it that children went to church on Sunday, even if they didn't go themselves.'

STANLEY LOVELL

'In Harrold there was a certain amount of rivalry between the nonconformists and the Church of England, but whichever had the better outings became the most popular!

My father was not a bit religious, and thought the church

was on the side of the rich, but my mother was a devout woman. She read the lesson in church when she was ninety-five, on some special occasion. As a boy I had to go to church on a Sunday morning and to Sunday School, and church again at night, but once given the choice I stayed away.'

ARTHUR 'LOL' THEW

'Our family were big Methodists and we had our own pew in the Waterlow Road Chapel [Dunstable]. I did a lot of work for the Chapel, helping to raise funds for a new organ and heating. I was also Treasurer for a number of years.'

ERIC THORNE

'There are two churches in Thurleigh village, the Baptist and St. Peter's Church of England. I was church warden there for twenty-eight years, and when I retired my son John took over from me. My daughter plays the church organ and her husband is also a present church warden.'

JOHN 'JACK' THORNE

'At one time whilst I was teaching, the Chairman of the Governors and I fell out: he was the parson of the village, an old man and a bachelor. In those days there was no amusement for the village children and the chapel people bought a magic lantern show and I went to see it with the children. Since I was no longer in favour, I was not asked to the vicarage to tea any more! It was a privilege to be asked to the vicarage.

Working in a Church School you were expected to attend church. The school occasionally organised concerts and events but these had to have the approval of the vicar: they could not be held during religious festivals, lent, etc.

When I had held my teaching post for about two years it happened that I went to a display given by a newly-formed Boys' Club. I was very impressed and told my boys about it. They asked if they could have a similar one so I made inquiries and was well on the way to arranging it when I had *a visit from the local vicar who was also Chairman of the School Managers. The following conversation ensured: "I hear you are thinking of forming a Boys' Club"' he said. I agreed that that was my intention, whereupon he replied "I don't wish you to do that: we don't want any innovations in the village", so I gave up the idea!'*

GLADYS WALLIS

'I was a Trustee of the local Jeffries and Harveys Charity [Thurleigh]. Rents from land and the old Red Lion went into the coffers of this charity and this money was distributed to the poorest of the poor on Christmas Day. They had to attend church, and it was distributed by the vicar and the Foundation Trustee and Lord of the Manor, Squire Thomson. Having received their church money, some were observed to make a rapid departure through the bottom gate of the church, and a quick dash for the pub. It was Christmas, after all!'

FREDERICK WILDMAN

'It is obvious that the church's three hundred seats were always occupied until about 1912. The choir numbered fifteen to twenty and, I was informed by an ex-member of the choir, that boys were paid the sum of 1/- (5p) per quarter for their melodious efforts. One section of the church seats was filled by "Men only", another by "Women only" and the remainder by "Children only" due to some peculiar custom of the time. It appears that, after the buses started to run through the village, the numbers attending church started a steady decline and this tendency was accelerated still further after the "Wireless" was made available to the people in 1922 and, we are all aware of the fact that, since the introduction of Television, congregations have fallen alarmingly to less than twenty per service. It is also known that the same attendance figures apply to the chapel. It is not that people are much less "Godly" but that there are so many other attractions on a Sunday.'

H. S. BROWN

'Along St. Lloyes [in Bedford], opposite the prison, where there are now shops, stood a row of p'haps eight almshouses for members of St. Paul's Church. Two high steps led up into these cottages. Elderly people were housed there and given one shilling and a loaf of bread a week. These were spinsters and elderly church patrons. I had a great aunt living there and when I was about twelve years of age I used to take her a Sunday dinner and read to her from the Bible, as she was bed-ridden then. My aunt, Miss Litchfield, could tell some tales. I can picture her now in her lace cuffs and lace bonnet – which reminded me of a cake doily, – with her buttoned felt boots with little neat buttons and a button hook which I used to do them up.

Next door to the prison there were also a row of almshouses, which have since disappeared. These stood between the church and the prison, on the site where Bedford High School was later built.'

EDITH 'IRENE' CORNWELL

The Priory Church, Dunstable, focal point for worship, social and educational activities, a meeting point for members of the community, playing an active role in enforcing standards of morality and in facilitating social cohesion. The role of the church within the community in both town and country was important, influential and regulatory, prior to the invasory effects of the media, particularly television.
Photo: Luton & Neighbourhood Illustated, publisher T G Hobbs.

'We had meetings [in Dunstable] in the week connected with the church: it was known as the "chapel" – nonconformists called theirs the chapel. I was in the Band of Hope, and we had socials and there was a little library. We went to Ashridge once a year for an outing, and were taken in a waggonette, a horse-drawn open vehicle with seats back-to-back. We called cars "smelly things" when they first came about.'

ELSIE ENGLAND

THE BIG HOUSE

THE BIG HOUSE

Introduction

As Britain entered the Edwardian era, many country estates were in evidence, owned by the titled aristocracy and by the gentry. Since the onset of the Industrial Revolution and the rise of the Middle Classes, rigid class distinctions were becoming less clearly defined, and many enterprising working-class families had, through their endeavours, 'purchased' a higher position in society. Wealthy families could emulate the gentry and elevate their position in society and in political life.

For Antiques, Curios, Pictures, and

Furniture of all Periods,

⟶ VISIT ⟶

H. Rixson,

Ye Olde Retreate, DUNSTABLE.

TELEPHONE No. 25.

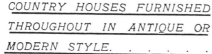

COUNTRY HOUSES FURNISHED THROUGHOUT IN ANTIQUE OR MODERN STYLE. . . . . .

Catering for the upper classes! From Year Book and Directory, 1913. Published by Miles Taylor and printed by the Dunstable Gazette.

Through strong religious belief and according to tradition, many people readily – sometimes grudgingly – accepted their lower status in life, and regarded the wealthy with deference. Staff were proud to be associated with their landed employers: the more powerful the employer, the more prestige attaching to their staff.

Many of the wealthy families were generous benefactors, and took a genuine interest in the welfare of local people. They were patrons, offering support for charitable initiatives. Owners of the 'big houses' and the estates which went with them, could offer employment on the land, accommodation in estate cottages, and educational facilities (the gentry and the clergy were normally represented on governing bodies). Most employed a large domestic staff of butler, housekeeper, cooks, maids, governess, gardeners, horsekeepers, and chauffeur.

The large houses were almost industries, their vast acreages producing agricultural crops for marketing, and vegetables for the table, tended with care in the extensive kitchen gardens. Meat and dairy produce were plentiful, since most estates included facilities for animal rearing and dairy herd. Flowers for decoration of the grounds and the house were grown in abundance, and a selection would be dried for winter decoration. Before the age of public transport and mechanised vehicles, a range of horse-drawn vehicles were maintained, which meant extensive stabling facilities for horses for this purpose and for riding for pleasure.

From early morning until late at night these houses buzzed with activity. The maids would be up early, cleaning out ashes from the previous day's fires, cleaning grates, re-lighting fires in the living rooms, and cleaning and dusting ready for occupation. The cooking range would be cleared, relaid, black-leaded and lit, and breakfast prepared. After taking around water for washing, and early-morning tea, the Lady's Maid and the Gentleman's Valet would assist with dressing. There was breakfast to be served, and with the family up, pots to be emptied (usually in farm houses, less likely to be used in the larger houses), bedrooms to be cleaned and beds made up. The Housekeeper would instruct the staff on the daily tasks to be attended to, and all would go about their work. Cook and her staff would spend hours in the kitchen preparing breakfast, lunch, and dinner, cooking lavish dishes from traditional recipes (often memorised). No pre-packed and instant foods! Often butter and cheese were made by the kitchen staff, and animals skinned or plucked and cleaned, dressed, and prepared for cooking. During the day fires would need to be tended, meals served and so on. Many of the household staff would be provided with meals. The nurse and governess would be attending to the children, in the day nursery and school room, since it was customary for children to live apart from their parents. Children were normally invited to take their meals with their parents on occasions, and often the children would meet their parents at a set time of the day for a brief period, being returned to the nursery and the nursery staff, who usually slept in rooms adjoining the children's bedrooms. Thus, an army of staff would support the establishment, working late into the evening and usually 'living in'. If the family went away – for instance, shooting in Scotland – many of the staff accompanied them. This was a wonderful experience: one hears tell of members of staff who were themselves treated to breakfast in bed at such times! It was a thrilling experience for many ordinary country people. Some travelled by train, some by boat.

Foreign competition in food production had been increasing since the 1870s, with imports of corn from America, grown in abundance on the prairies. This came about also, because of improved methods of transportation. Since the 1880s refrigeration became possible and this facilitated the importation of meat. Crop prices in this country fell drastically. Tenant farmers were frequently unable to pay rents and many farmers went bankrupt. In 1917 the Corn Act was passed, to guarantee prices, but this was repealed a year later.

Even though many of the Bedfordshire estates fell on hard times – in particular between the wars, and this resulted in the sale of land and property – the families are not forgotten by the communities on which they once had considerable influence.

The Big House at Wootton

One such family is still remembered by the people of Wootton village. Newcomers to the locality may well have observed the fine old country house known as Wootton House, and reflected on its past, and that of those who owned and resided at the house. One of the longest-surviving members of the original owners of Wootton House – and indeed, much of the surrounding area – is Mrs Pelham Reid.

The Family

Eyvor Sibyl Pelham Reid, (neé Doyne-Ditmas), a lady of some distinction, was born in India on 11 February 1908, whilst her father, a Major in the Royal Field Artillery, was serving in India. Her maternal grandfather, Sir Phillip Monoux Payne, who farmed at Bourne End until his death in 1935, was a well-known North Bedfordshire landowner and country gentleman. The family are descended from wealthy land-owning gentry, and are able to trace their ancestry back to the Middle Ages. At one point in time, the family 'manor' included most of the land at Wootton and the surrounding area. This Wootton 'manor' had belonged to the Monoux family since the sixteenth century. The Payne branch of the family owned large areas of land at Tempsford and Blunham, and property which included Blunham House. They also owned a considerable amount of property in the West Indies where the name survives (*viz* Payne Bay).

There were seven children born of Major and Mrs Doyne Ditmas, – daughter of Sir Phillip Payne – Eyvor, Nancy (Ilean), Myra, Phillip, Derek, Sibyl and Harrold. In keeping with Victorian and Edwardian family traditions, Eyvor, being the eldest daughter, assumed responsibility for the others, fulfilling mother's role. 'My mother was always keen to delegate her parental responsibilities to paid servants'. The warmth, affection and attention which all children need and crave in childhood, Eyvor maintains she gained through her close relationship with her father whom she describes as a most kind, caring and understanding person. it was father who crept up to the children's room after the servants had sent them to bed: 'He would tuck us up and slip a little sweet under our pillow if he thought we had had a bad day'.

Eyvor is very fond of children, and actually set up and manned a clinic for local children in the West Indies, where she stayed during the winters, after her marriage. 'You know, the history books give rather a misleading impression of life in the colonies, in that they never mention the loyalties which existed between us and the local people. I can recall a time just after Independence, when I organised a dinner for some local dignitaries. My black staff were very upset about it and thought it quite wrong for me to entertain black people in my home. I have never tasted such awful food as that which they prepared for us on that occasion! It must be said that we cared for the people whom we employed, and they cared for us. They respected us, and depended on us as we in turn depended on them.'

During the first world war, whilst the Major was abroad, and Wootton House was occupied by Col. the Hon. Robert Villiers Dillon, RHA, MP, Mrs Doyne-Ditmas and her children lived in a rented property at Great Linford, now part of the Milton Keynes development. This temporary home of theirs was gutted by fire, and Eyvor recalls that they were lucky to escape without injury. They then moved to the Manor at Newport Pagnell, until Wootton House became vacant.

After the war Eyvor's parents took up residence at Wootton

Wootton House, a splendid William and Mary House and country residence, set in the village of Wootton.
Photo: courtesy Allot and Barnard and Knight, Frank & Rutley.

The fine oak staircase at Wootton House. Photo: courtesy Allot and Barnard and Knight, Frank & Rutley.

House, which is a fine and imposing William and Mary Country House built in the late 17th century, and being part of the family estate. This is situated close to the Parish Church of St. Mary, to the west of the village. Many members of the family are buried at St. Mary's including Eyvor's grandmother, Lady Payne, who died just after the first world war following a riding accident. After her death, Sir Phillip, Eyvor's grandfather, moved to Bourne End House until his death, and he too is buried at St. Mary's. One window in the church was installed by the family and is dedicated to the memory of Eyvor's mother's brother, Humphrey, who died in infancy.

The floor of Wootton Church chancel is almost entirely paved with memorial slabs commemorating the Monoux family. The oldest of these is dated 1675 and is in memory of Sir Humphrey Monoux. A second monument to Sir Humphrey appears in marble on the north wall, dated 1680. Opposite is a memorial to his son Phillip, dated 1707.

The Staff

Whilst living at Wootton House Eyvor's mother employed a large domestic staff which included cooks, chauffeurs, maids, gardeners, grooms, nannies and nurses to care for the children. A Governess had the responsibility of educating the children. As was customary, the children were later sent to boarding school and Eyvor went to Beaconsfield and then to Crescent House Ladies College in Linden Road, Bedford. College advertisements appearing in 'Bedford and Bedford Schools' reveal that 'The practice of speaking French all day is enforced'! After leaving, Eyvor attended Gloucester School of Economics for one year, leaving at the age of seventeen. She was not allowed to work, as her mother felt it inappropriate for her to occupy a job of work which could be filled by someone with greater need of income.

Good Times

Eyvor was given a car for her seventeenth birthday by her father, who was a keen motorist and a founder member of the Bedfordshire Motor Club. 'Father treated me as a boy, and even taught me to ride a motorbike when I was fourteen. He gave me faith in my ability to do things, and this gave me confidence. I feel that I benefitted greatly from this upbringing and from his influence.' She also enjoyed hunting and beagling, which is the hunting of hares on foot. Father was a keen horseman and the family hunted with the Oakley and Whaddon Hunts. Eyvor had been making clothes for her sisters since the age of twelve, and she subsequently took up dress-designing, did exhibition dancing at the Savoy, and prior to that, taught dancing with her dance tutor, Miss Stewart, at the Crofton Rooms in St. Cuthbert's Bedford. Another of her pastimes was knitting, which she was taught at the age of four, and which she has done ever since.

The Bedfordshire Motor Club at Silsoe, c. 1910 of which Eyvor's father was a founder member.
Photo: Luton & Neighbourhood Illustrated, publisher T G Hobbs.

Whilst at Wootton House, Major Doyne-Ditmas installed a platten engine to produce electricity. At this time the grand old house was bustling with activity. The servants were accommodated in the extensive attic rooms, and a stable block housed the Major's treasured horses. However, as the family's income from farming diminished, due in part to the agricultural depression which had begun in the late nineteenth century, it became necessary to sell off family assets.

Depressed Times

In 1927 Wootton House was sold. Following the sale of their home, the family moved to Kempston Manor, from where Eyvor was married in February 1929. Ownership of Wootton House then passed to several families of repute.

In the first instance the property was sold to The Rt. Hon William G A Ormsby-Gore MP, and Lady Beatrice, and subsequently to Col. and Mrs Morgan Grenville, JP and Magistrate. During their ownership of the house it was used

Major and Mrs Doyne Ditmus and family in 1930.

Pictured in 1932, four generations of the family at Kempston Manor, Sir Phillip Monoux Payne, Mrs Sibyl Doyne Ditmus, Eyvor and son.

by the French Resistance who occupied the upper part of the property. A local resident, one-time domestic at the house, remembers that matting was put on the wooden stairway to protect the polished oak surface from the soldiers' boots. Low-flying aircraft are known to have dropped onto the lawns, goods and messages to the French, and there are those who still recall occasions when pandemonium broke out as the French stampeded onto the roof as aircraft flew overhead!

Later owners were Mr and Mrs Quentin Crewe and their daughter. He was a friend of Princess Margaret, and she occasionally visited him at Wootton House. He is thought to have been a journalist and author, and to have suffered from muscular dystrophe. His wife was a TV presenter at one time. She has maintained her contact with the Wootton ladies whom she employed whilst living at Wootton House.

In more recent times the Listed building has been in the

possession of local property developers. It is temporarily and carefully converted to be used as office accommodation, as is the stable block. However, in spite of the many changes the house has seen over the years, the family picture of the Oakley Hunt assembled at Wootton House continues to hang in its rightful place above the large redbrick open fireplace in the entrance hall, which contains its original stone flagged floor and panelled dado. In the servants' quarters are still to be seen the original cupboards which bear labels proclaiming 'pillows', 'maids', 'bathtowels', 'lavatory' and so on.

When the family estates were broken up after the second world war, each of the children acquired property and land. Eyvor was given Wood Farm, at Wood End, Wootton. Having spent several years at Vine Cottage, Wood End, she moved into the farmhouse in 1959 and remained there until 1974, at which time she moved to Emberton in Buckinghamshire.

Eyvor's first husband lost his life in the second world war, and she re-married in 1944. Her second husband, Major Pelham-Reid, was a pig-breeder, and became an authority on intensive pig farming. Theirs was the largest experimental farm in England at that time, using antibiotics. They were among the first use a Combine Harvester, which they had brought over from Canada. The couple had their own light aircraft and were well-known local characters. Eyvor herself was an important political figure, involved with Mid Bedfordshire Conservatives for many years, and also a Parish Councillor.

After the break-up of the estate, Eyvor's mother, Sibyl Monoux Doyne Ditmus, came to own, among other things, a group of seventeenth century estate cottages in Cause End Road, Wootton, including Warren Cottage, and it was at Cause End Cottage where she resided, following the death of her husband until just before her own death. She was a respected and well-known member of the village community, who was frequently to be seen riding her 'sit-up-and-beg' bicycle around the village. She made a point of regularly visiting the people whom she had employed in the past, and kept in touch with their families, even in the latter years of her life. She was President of the Wootton Women's Institute for many years, and was instrumental in organising many war-time activities, including 'Gift day Sale – proceeds to the boys of the village now serving with HM Forces – for Xmas'. Despite her wealth and influence, she will long be remembered with affection, as a caring member of the community.

As is apparent at Wootton House and St. Mary's Church, the family influence in this community still survives and will do so for many years to come. It is pleasing to see that the Monoux name has now been given to a newly-created street, leading to a small housing development in the centre of the village.

Village Folk Reminisce

'Wootton House was a short distance up the road from the bakery where I worked all my life. This house belonged to Sir Phillip Payne. Sir Phillip used to come to church every Sunday. He was a short fellow, used to enter by the back door and sat in the rectory. Everything belonged to Sir Phillip, most of the land and the three farms in Wootton, rented to tenant farmers – the Frossels and Chennels. Bourne End was his farm and his house remains there, though much of the land has been sold. He had a foreman and two or three other workmen on the land. Because most of the land was privately owned by him, shooting and trapping weren't allowed. There was no common land around Wootton, for miles. The squire and his family were keen hunters, and members of the Oakley Hunt. They occasionally met at Wootton House, The Swan at Bromham and other places, and anyone could follow, on foot.

Vine Cottages at Wood End were Sir Phillip's labourers' cottages, and in more recent times Mrs Pelham Reid, his granddaughter, lived there. She moved there from Wood Farm, Wootton Green. Andrew Newbury and Mark Hutching were the two men who lived in these cottages for years. Members of Sir Phillip's family lived at Kempston, then the big house at Box End, and his daughter, Mrs Doyne Ditmus, after the death of her husband, Major Ditmus, finally lived at Cause End Cottage. All of these estate cottages and much of their land has now been sold, I believe. 56 Cause End Road was an estate cottage occupied by George and Lisa Lowe, who had five sons and a daughter. It was later occupied by Rosy and Jim Keech. They lived there for many years, opposite the cottage where I was born. After Rosy died Jim moved in with his son. He was about ninety when he died and was always a farm worker. He kept poultry at the cottage and would glean all day to get corn for these hens, and you'd often see him walking to Bedford market with the hens in a basket. Archie and Vera Clark lived there for many years too. He worked at London Brick. They were divorced and Vera married Vic Caves from the shop. George Lowe's son, Dicky, lived at 54 Cause End Road for many years. He was groomsman for Sir Phillip Payne and drove his pony and trap. After him it was occupied by Mr Parker.

I knew Mrs Doyne Ditmus and Sir Phillip Payne, her father. She was a keen cyclist and used to cycle to Clapham and other areas, visiting people she knew – many were people who had worked for her in earlier times. She was prone to accidents on her bike and was often seen with a bruised and blackened face, after a cycling mishap, but she went on undeterred, pushing her pedals around the village.

It is sad that much of the original village is vanishing and housing developments are spoiling the village. There is talk of demolishing old Wootton School, built for the village children in 1877 by Sir Phillip Payne. Few of the old cottages remain, the old lock-up which stood outside the church has gone, as have the village stocks, called the 'pound' which stood outside Mr Redman's cottage in Bedford Road: he was the Wheelwright and Undertaker. His wife still lives there.

At one time Wootton House was occupied by the Dillons, who employed three gardeners – Fred Pateman, Joe Green and a chap called Ellis. They had no cars then but employed

Geoff Mepham, Headteacher's son, Wootton School, and member of the Blue Cross football team.

a groomsman and coachman to take care of the horses and traps. Joe was the coachman, an Irish fellow. Colonel Dillon was elderly and retired and they had a lot of servants and it was the Lady's Maid who became my employer's wife. They had a son, Bill, who is the present owner of the Wootton Riding and Livery Stables just down the road from Wootton House.'

FREDERICK BURRAWAY

'The old school was built after the 1870 Education Act was passed. It was given us by a man who lived at Top Farm, Sir Phillip Payne. He gave the land and school to the County Council to be used for education purposes for as long as they wanted it. There was another school adjoining the Cock Inn, the Infants School. We went there for several years and then went to the big school (Wootton Primary), which is now boarded up. Sir Phillip's granddaughter, Mrs Pelham Reid, well her husband flew his own aeroplane. Her father was a typical army man. Sir Phillip's daughter, Mrs Doyne Ditmus, she was a blood donor for a number of years, used to ride about on her cycle. "Squire of the Parish" was Sir Phillip, he didn't come about the village much. I was learning bell ringing and I've been there when he's come in and sat in the chancery. He owned most of Wootton.'

STANLEY LOVELL

'Christmas celebrations in the village during my childhood included carol singing at Wootton House, where the carol singers were invited in for mince pies and sherry. The owners at that time were Major and Mrs Doyne Ditmus. It was Mrs Doyne Ditmus's father, Sir Phillip Payne, who funded the building of Wootton School for the education of local children. Everyone knew this family, who were the local gentry.'

CONSTANCE ROBINSON

Another beautiful family home – the Wardown Mansion in Luton – built in 1877. The Mansion and grounds, comprising approximately fifty acres of parkland – formerly known as Bramingham Shott – was acquired by the Town Council and is now the Luton Museum. Photo: Luton & Neighbour-hood Illustrated, publisher T G Hobbs.

The Big House at Sharnbrook

'I went to work for Mrs Allen of the engineering company, whose home was at Turvey. It was very hard work, starting 5.30am and cleaning the flues out and getting the range going red hot so the toast could be done over it at 7.00am. I often got the back of my hands rapped with a handbrush if it wasn't ready in time. I was kitchen maid. I had to clean, get rabbits ready, chickens picked and so on. I was courting then, and my

*Colworth House in the 1930s. Reproduced by permission of the
Bedfordshire Magazine. Photo: courtesy Michael Jones.*

boyfriend wanted me to go to Sharnbrook, which I did,
working for Sir Albert and Lady Bowen at Colworth House,
Sharnbrook.

There were fifteen staff at Colworth House, butler and
housekeeper. I went as scullery maid. Sir Albert had business
in London I think, but they also had a big estate and farms.
There was a "bothy" where eight or nine gardening boys lived.
This was a part of the house. It was like a lodge but bigger.
The head gardener had his own house.

Sir Albert died soon after I started working at Colworth
House, and the domestic staff were given the opportunity of
moving to the London house to work for Lady Bowen. Some of
the staff went but I decided to stay, as I didn't was to leave my
boyfriend!

The Bowen family have an interesting history you know.
Colworth House belongs to Unilevers now. One of my sons
worked there for thirty years as a gardener and still lives in
North Lodge.'

GWENDOLINE BROWN

Albert Bowen was born at Staffordshire in 1858, his mother being a descendant of Wedgwood the potters. Albert became an engineer and was President of the Southern Railway which established rail routes from Buenos Aires through the Andes to Valpariso. He married Alice Anita Crowther in 1884 and they raised four of their children (Edward, Winifred, Gertrude and Evelyn) in Buenos Aires. The fifth child, (Harold), was born in London after their return to England.

Sir Albert was a JP and High Sheriff of Bedford. At Colworth the family rode to hounds and took part in many diverse local activities. The whole family enjoyed an exciting social life, and entertained many visitors. A stage was built in Colworth House during Harold's childhood, and the children gave theatrical performances to local audiences.

The Bowen family were intellectual, artistic, well-travelled and extremely well connected (to mention just one name, Lord St. Just, Governor of the Bank of England).

Harold married Vera Donnet, daughter of a prosperous Ukranian businessman, and the couple set up home at 2 Spanish Place, Mayfair in 1923. Her mother is said to have been a favourite of the Czar, and so there were noble connections. Vera became an expert on the ballet; Harold was an artist, poet and musician.

After Sir Albert's death in 1924 his eldest son, Edward, settled in Gloucestershire. Alice, Lady Bowen, wished to live in London and bought 37 Cadogan Gardens where she was to remain until her death in 1943. Harold and Vera became the new owners of Colworth House, but neither had the knowledge or training to successfully manage an estate. Harold did have a deep affection for the house where he had spent so many very happy years, and for a while his enjoyment of the house continued. Many of the couple's artistic friends, including those connected with the ballet and the world of art, visited the house at weekends. Their son Nicholas lived there with his nanny, Miss Godfrey, whilst his parents attended to their commitments in London during the week.

By 1928 the estate was losing money. Having had one miscarriage, Vera was again pregnant, and it is thought that she persuaded her husband, Harold, to move away from the countryside. the house was then sold. The estate, which extended to some 2,200 acres in 1920, had by 1930 been divided into some fifty units, and disposed of.

During happier times, Sir Albert planted an oak tree for each of his grandchildren in a circle around the house in the home park. Shortly after the war Harold and his son, Wing Commander Nicholas, were appalled to see that the trees planted for John Bowen, (Edward's son, killed motor racing in 1939), Bille Cobbe (son of Winifred and Lt. Col. Alexander Stanhoppe Cobbe, VC DSO, killed in the Battle of Britain) and Peter Cornwallis (son of Gertrude and Kinahan Cornwallis, CMG CBE DSO, killed in a bomber command raid on Germany in the last days of the war), had all withered, as though in sympathy for the death of those for whom they had been planted.

MR M JONES / MR N BOWEN

The Big House at Old Warden

One cannot pass through Old Warden without observing the very large and imposing stone mansion and former home of the Shuttleworths, built on the site of a previous mansion by Joseph Shuttleworth, and being a replica of Gawthorpe Hall in Lancashire.

Richard Ormonde Shuttleworth, grandson of Joseph Shuttleworth, was the last squire of the Old Warden Estate. He and his family will be long-remembered: his mother established The Richard Ormonde Shuttleworth Remembrance Trust in 1944, which includes the estate, the Shuttleworth Collection and the Mansion, which is a part of Shuttleworth College. The Collection attracts visitors and aircraft enthusiasts from around the world.

The Shuttleworth's family home at Old Warden, built by Richard's
grandfather, Joseph Shuttleworth, in 1872.
Photo reproduced by permission of Jane's Information Group from
Richard O Shuttleworth.

'The Shuttleworths came from Lincoln, where they made farm
machinery, steam traction engines and so on. The founder of
this business, Joseph, who purchased the Old Warden Estate
in 1872, had two sons, Alfred and Frank. When Joseph
Shuttleworth died, Alfred inherited the business, and Frank
the estate. Frank married late in life and had one son, Richard
Shuttleworth, born 1909. Alfred had no children. When they
died, Frank and Alfred left a considerable amount of money to
Richard, the estate being valued at two million pounds in
1913, and this was held in trust until Richard reached the age
of twenty-three in 1932. His inheritance included the Old
Warden Estate and a great deal of land at Goldington Bury, to
the east of Bedford, known as the Goldington Estate. The
whole of that land at Goldington was sold to pay the death
duties on Richard Shuttleworth's estate when he died.

Richard Shuttleworth, born 1909, photographed by Lallie Charles, Edwardian portrait photographer. Photo reproduced by permission of Jane's Information Group from Richard O Shuttleworth.

Richard was the only Shuttleworth child, and his father died in 1913 when he was four. He was quite a unique person, and was a very dear friend of mine, a great companion and extremely kind and generous to me. We met in 1925, at the famous Academy for Further Education known as Crammers, at Lathbury Park in Newport Pagnell, about sixteen miles from Old Warden, which was run by Col. William Trevor. Richard and I had both attended public school and were hopeful of passing examinations in order to obtain commissions in the army. I am thankful to say that I did not pass my examinations. Richard did, and went on to Sandhurst and I eventually went to Faraday House Electrical Engineering College which was in Southampton Row, Bloomsbury, London, for a four-year course leading to the award of "The Faraday House Diploma". It does not exist now but was a wonderful basic training for engineering.

When we were at Lathbury, Richard and I met over a motorbike which he possessed. It wasn't a powerful machine at all but he had dismantled it and dropped the pieces in amongst some chaff in a barn which was also used as a hen house. We had to sift the chaff in order to find the pieces, which we eventually did. We were not allowed motorbikes, but several of us had them and we kept them in the nearby village of Sherrington. Crammers was a private educational establishment for examination coaching, run by Col Trevor, a remarkable man. There were twenty-eight pupils and fourteen, including Richard, had been Etonians. I had been at Uppingham. Richard entered the Supplementary Reserve of 16th/5th Lancer Regiment in 1927 and was commissioned in 1930 and posted to Colinton, Midlothian, among other places. He was very keen on point-to-point racing and rode his horses much in the same style as he rode his motorbike – flat out. During this period, Richard and I kept in touch.

Later on Richard took to Motor racing and achieved a good deal of success in races at Brooklands, Donington Park and elsewhere. I went with him as his mechanic in the Ulster TT in an Aston Martin. Unfortunately the engines from Aston Martin at that time were fitted with an electron plate on which the valve gear was mounted. One of the lugs holding a valve rocker spindle broke away and put us out of the race on the 13th lap. Richard was always kindness itself, although at times he used to explode, but it was over in a very short time. This was one such occasion! He bought an Arrow Aster super-charged, sleeve valved, open tourer when he was still in the army. He had a very close rapport with the Arrol Aster Company in Dumphries, and particularly the Works Foreman. By that time he had started collecting old motor cars. Richard asked his friend, the Foreman at Arrol Asters, if he knew of any man, possibly retired, who would be prepared to come down to Old Warden and work on and look after the old cars. The Foreman suggested that a man called George Hackett would be suitable. Asked where he could find him,

Richard driving a Bugatti in the 1933 Mannin Moar race in Douglas, Isle of Man. Photo reproduced by permission of Jane's Information Group from Richard O Shuttleworth.

Richard participating in the 261-mile International Trophy, May 1935. Drivers included Sir Malcolm Campbell.
Photo reproduced by permission of Jane's Information Group from Richard O Shuttleworth.

his friend replied "fishing by the canal", so Richard went up the canal until he found him and offered him the job, which George willingly accepted. Richard wanted him to come immediately and offered to take his things, many of which were pawned! Armed with the pawn tickets, he retrieved George's possessions, loaded them into his sports Arrol Aster, and drove him back to Old Warden where he was given a cottage to live in and Mrs Shuttleworth did it up for him inside and made him comfortable. The action was typical of both of them.

On one occasion an old chap who had worked for Richard's father called to get a pair of wheels as he had become too old to manage to carry his crop of potatoes from his allotment and had no way of transporting them. Richard told him, rather abruptly, to call back in a week or so, and then promptly sorted out some old aircraft wheels and spent the whole week making him a cart!

Following the dealth of her son in 1940, Mrs Shuttleworth organised, on behalf of the Bedfordshire Red Cross, a convalescent, and anxilliary hospital at her home. Photo reproduced by permission of Jane's Information Group from Richard O Shuttleworth.

Richard had taken a keen interest in farming and in the management of his estate and Mrs Shuttleworth, Richard's mother, started Shuttleworth College in memory of her son, who died in 1940. The Trust which she set up, also includes the Shuttleworth Collection. The Mansion has survived very much in its original condition, and is now used mainly for administrative and study purposes, with student accommodation on the top floor. It is a part of Shuttleworth College and has retained its character and atmosphere as Mrs Shuttleworth intended. She herself died in 1968.'

JIMMY EDMUNDS

The Squires

It was common for the Squire and Lord of the Manor to have private chapels in the local church, with manorial pews for his family (occasionally with heating facilities).

The church was maintained by way of tithes paid by local people, which amounted to one-tenth of a person's income. The Squire also played a large part in providing for the upkeep of the church.

The local Squire was the pillar of society, a person of considerable social standing and regarded with esteem. He would have extensive farming interests and land- and property-holdings which included farms, tenanted properties and livestock. His home would be staffed by local people, usually, including a butler, housekeeper, housemaids, cook and kitchen maids, coachman/horsekeeper, and gardener.

As a result of the agricultural depression, (1880–1930), changes in tax laws and other factors, by the turn of the century many country squires were in financial difficulty but some such families held on to their estates until well into the 1920s.

The Squire was often a generous benefactor within the community. His family had been associated with local village families over many generations, and the Squire often took a genuine interest in the local people and possessed a strong sense of duty towards the community as a whole. Some built model villages, and provided estate cottages for workers, and accommodation for retired workers. Village schools were often funded by the Squire. The relationship between the Squire and the local people ensured continuity and stability in the common bond they shared through dependence on the land.

During the war, many of the large houses were used as hospitals or for the convalescing war wounded. Some were commandeered for use by the Forces. Others were converted into Care Homes for the terminally ill and for the elderly, or hospitals for the mentally ill: others have in recent times, been put to commercial usage or converted for residential use. Luton acquired its museum in this manner. One home became part of an educational and historic trust.

Duke Herbrand's wife was known as the Flying Duchess. She suffered from head noises and was very deaf but nevertheless took up flying when in her sixties and did record

Woburn Cottage Hospital, founded by Mary, Duchess of Bedford c. 1910, now the Maryland Adult Education College.
Photo: courtesy Mr S Houfe & Mr J Lowe.

flights to India and Africa. She was interested in hospitals, and the Duke built her one which was known as Maryland: she was known there as Sister Mary. She was a good sports woman, fisherwoman, rider, and keen ornothologist. She set the boys at the local school competitions on birds and provided clothing and took them around on her yacht. They became her footmen or chauffeurs, some of them. She used to take them down to Devonshire: at one time you could walk from Buckinghamshire to the Wash without leaving their land. They used Battlesden House for airmen convalescing during the war, and this became a home for Sister Livesy who was the Matron at Maryland, in her retirement.

The Duchess is said by local people to have been very autocratic and prone to shocking rages. She was a fresh-air fiend and would go around opening all the windows in the house, with her husband in pursuit, closing them.

Years ago, there used to be a large oak along the approach road to the house [Woburn Abbey], that marked the boundary of Bedfordshire and Buckinghamshire and it is worth recording an unusual happening that used to take place there.

It is said that the Duke (Squire) very strongly forbade the acceptance of 'tips' from visitors by his staff. However, a frequent visitor was a gentleman who ran a famous zoo near Hamburg, and came over to help the Squire with his collection of animals. As he approached the Boundary Oak he would tap the chauffeur sent to collect him on the shoulder and pass an envelope to him. No word was spoken and this ritual was continued in reverse order on returning to the station via the oak!

Some landowners had the reputation of being very autocratic. Local people maintain that one such individual was the same Duke Herbrand, who died in 1940. His policy was to purchase land and enclose it within the park. Battlesden Manor, built in 1864 on the outskirts of Battlesden village near Woburn, by Sir Joseph Paxton who built Crystal Palace, was purchased by the Duke in 1885 and demolished, along with other local properties. This had been a splendid Elizabethan house built for Sir Edward Page-Turner. On another occasion he engaged in debate in the House of Lords – allegedly not altogether for altruistic reasons – concerning the tax on bricks, which effectively meant that poor people could not afford to build. The law was subsequently rescinded, creating a particularly opportune moment to build a twelve-mile long wall around the park. Many are still of the opinion that 'the Duke did not wish to have a community living nearby, other than his staff. If you saw him in the park you had to get behind a tree so he didn't see you'. 'You had to touch your cap to him and he just about had the strength to put his hand up.'

The Benefactors

Many local family names are synonymous with philanthropic activities, probably the most well-known being the Harpurs, whose educational endowment has for centuries, provided a service renoun for its excellence, enabling children from all classes of society, to receive tuition of the highest standard. Other names, from among the middle classes, the gentry and nobility, also spring to mind when one considers commitment to community service:

the Howards of Kempston, founders of
   the Britannia Iron Works;
the Lukes of Pavenham and Odell;
the Polhills of Bedford;
the Russells of Ampthill;
the Wernhers of Luton Hoo;
the Wells of Felmersham and Bedford, brewers;
the Shuttleworths of Old Warden;
the Wingfields of Ampthill;
the Whitbreads of Cardington and Southill, brewers.

The more fortunate members of society, often devout Christians, have deemed service to the community and charitable acts, a religious duty. Social status confers responsibility for those less fortunate. Consider one name, in particular, that of the Allen family, formerly of Bromham House, now Bromham Hospital.

William Allen is best remembered as founder and Chairman of the firm of W H Allen, Son and Company Ltd., Queen's Engineering Works, Bedford, employing about 1,500 men. He took a deep interest in all that concerned the welfare of his employees, and in the various district charities.

William Henry Allen, JP, was born in 1844 and became Justice of the Peace for the county of Bedford in 1897, and High Sheriff of Bedfordshire in 1904. At this time the Memorial to the Soldiers who fell in the Boer war was unveiled in Bedford and Princess Christian was also received in Bedford on the occasion of the opening of an exhibition (the first time that Royalty had honoured the town with a visit), and a presentation of plate and a silver shield was made to the cruiser bearing the county name. William Allen was Visiting Magistrate of the County Gaol, a member of the Reformatory Committee, President of the Bedford Musical Society, Chairman of the Bedfordshire Automobile Club, Liveryman of the Worshipful Company of Musicians, Freeman of the City of London, member of the Royal Institution, member of Council of the Institution of Mechanical Engineers, member of the Institutions of Civil Engineers, Naval Architects and Electrical Engineers, Fellow of Royal Geographical, Royal Colonial Institute, and Statistical Societies.

Whilst High Sheriff of Bedfordshire, William Allen wrote a book: The Shrievalty of the County of Bedford 1904–1905, in which he details duties undertaken by him during this period, and comments that 'the position provides the opportunity of promoting the interests of humanitarian

William H Allen, JP.
'Contemporary Biographies'
courtesy County Record Office.

The High Sheriff's carriage in front of Bromham House during the
Shrievalty of W H Allen, JP 1904–05. Mr Allen and his chaplain, the
Rev. C W Browning of Bromham, are about to enter the coach.
Photo: courtesy of Mr S Houfe & Mrs I Newman.

causes, initiating and directing movements such as that which led to associating the county with the warship of its name, and of popularising – if needs were – the best forms of national sport, public and social functions'.

Occupants of all the 'big houses' had a part to play in the welfare of local people, and after the Great War many opened their homes to convalescing soldiers. The Duke of Bedford built Maryland for his wife Mary, the 'Flying Duchess' a hospital for the war-wounded. Mary also took a keen interest in the welfare of local children, some of whom accompanied her on holidays. Some land-owners funded the building of schools, and financed church restoration, many were school governors, some were active in the Women's Institute movements. Many members of the middle classes and the landed gentry were aldermen or members of parliament, and many took a keen interest in community life and served on local committees. One name which may be familiar in Dunstable is that of Edwin Timms, a member of the Dunstable Borough Council, Alderman, Mayor, Deputy Mayor, Governor of Chew Foundation Charity, who served on the Food Control Committee for Dunstable during the Great War.

Familiar in the Ampthill area is the name of Anthony Wingfield, who was active in local and political life as Chairman of Quarter Sessions and Deputy Lieutenant and Justice of the Peace for the county of Bedford, Chairman of Visiting Magistrates for Prison, Member of the Council of Zoological Society of London, High Sheriff of Bedford, and Chairman of Mid Bedfordshire Conservative Association.

In addition to managing large country estates and supervising a substantial workforce in the process, and often attending to other business interests, these pillars of society still found time to take an interest in, and promote the welfare of local people.

Another name, familiar to all, is that of Wells. Wing Commander Oliver Wells was awarded an OBE in the 1992

New Year Honours' List, for services to the community in Bedfordshire. He presents a most modest and unassuming character. Speaking of his family's connections with the Shuttleworths, for example, (he is Aviation Trustee for the Shuttleworth Collection, and his mother was a friend of Mrs Shuttleworth), he comments that 'they were rather grander than our family, with their large estate'. Assets of the Wells family business included (until rather recent changes) in the order of three hundred licensed premises!

Wing Commander Wells's grandfather, Charles Wells, is still remembered for having supported many local causes, including the County Hospital, the General Library, St. Paul's Church and the Board of Guardians. His sons, Col. Hayward and Sir Richard Wells, are also well-remembered in the county as most generous benefactors.

Charles Wells, founder of the local well-known brewery, and grandfather of Oliver Wells, pictured here as a young mid-shipman.
Photographed from an original picture by Mike Wells.
Courtesy Northampton Mercury Company Limited.

Life In Service: Echoes from the Past

It was less likely for boys to go into service, unless their fathers were employed in that capacity, but they were employed as Boot Boys or Kitchen Boys, fetching and carrying coal, water, etc., and gradually working their way up to the coveted post of Butler.

Staff took a pride in the work they did. There were benefits apart from pay, such as having one's own bedroom, and eiderdown, and having a bathroom. The servants' laundry was often sent out with household laundry, to be returned beautifully clean and pressed. If the family moved to a temporary residence the servants accompanied them, travelled first class by train, were met and transported by car to the house, served breakfast in bed. The servants enjoyed wonderful meals and had *their* quarters cleaned for them (the job of the 'third housemaid' – a part of the in-house training process).

A Children's Nurse

Irene, Children's Nurse.

'When I first left school I did some training with the Red Cross, to help in the hospital, and then worked as a child's nanny caring for an eight week old baby, for Major Badcock, the baby's grandfather, who lived at 10 Kimbolton Avenue [Bedford]. His daughter and husband lived with them, and she went out to business. I was there until the child, Ursula, reached the age of seven or eight years but when she was six she left for boarding school. My employers asked me to stay on to help the parlour maid. They had a cook, kitchen maid, parlour maid and myself. I stayed on there until I married.

I had to wear a uniform for work in them days, a navy coat, navy and white headcap, white cuffs and apron, navy frock. I had two nurseries, the day nursery and the night nursery, which I had to look after and keep clean. I took charge of the child's clothes, and sewed for her. The child's mother gave me a sheet from her bed which I made into a cot sheet as it was getting thin, and I put lace around the pillow slip and so on. I loved little Ursula, and we became very close.

It's marvellous really, when you look back, at the different lives of some children. You can understand, like with Princess Di, how they must love their nannies, you know, if they take to a nanny, which that child did. And it makes me think about it . . . I could do anything with that child really, she were very good, very good indeed. I used to have my nights off and I was courting then actually, and we used to laugh because the grandma she was very deaf and they never had 'earing aids you know, like they do now: they used to have these 'ere horn things like a trumpet . . . you know what I mean don't you? I always remember we used to die of laughing 'cos sometimes when it was my evening off and I used to have to be in by ten o'clock and I'd p'haps be a bit late and she'd be waiting for me in the kitchen entrance – waiting for me to come in. She'd say "Irene, do you know what the time is – you're late tonight" – "you're late" she'd say, 'cos they used to look after the child you see on the evenings when I was out, and that kind of thing. I used to have to shout the answer down this damned 'orn thing, and my husband could see it all through the kitchen window and he used to laugh like blazes.

One job I hated – detested – was turning down the beds at night and putting hot water bottles in. These were the stone ones with screw tops, and they were so 'eavy to take upstairs. There was a huge range for cooking in the kitchen and it looked lovely, shone – you could see your face in it. There was a clothes rack on a pulley for drying and airing clothes. I had to wash the baby's clothes by hand, of course. We had the most peculiar vacuum cleaner, sort of square thing, which had to be pumped. We called it the "old windbag". It did the job. I took over the butler's pantry, which is all the glasses and silver. Friday was the day for cleaning the silver on the kitchen table. We had a laugh when we were doing it. It was a general routine and we didn't make hard work of it. When I went for walks I took the baby to Bedford Park, where there were peacocks at that time. There used to be a bandstand floating on Bedford River, at one time.

When the baby was small and they were having company, I had to go to the bank to get out the best silver. The bank was opposite the arcade in the High Street. I fetched it on the pram as it was so heavy – tureens and so on.

When I helped serving meals for the family, when company came, I had to wear something different, fancy cuffs, black and white. I earned five shillings a week, plus board. You had to buy your aprons and cap out of this, get your shoes mended, and buy your stockings. I bought a Singer sewing machine for two shillings and sixpence a week, which I was very proud of. It is still going strong and my granddaughter has it now. The household one was complicated to use, a German make. I made dresses for little Ursula until she started school and then she had to have certain overalls and different things.

Mrs Badcock, the old grandma, was a faith healer – a spiritual healer. Sometimes, if the cook had a bad head and was feeling unwell, she healed her. She didn't believe in doctors. I must say the laying on of hands seemed to work.'

EDITH 'IRENE' CORNWELL

A Chauffeur/Gardener

'I was in nursery gardening for seven years, at Laxtons Nurseries in Polhill Avenue, Bedford, where the college now stands. During this seven years I got to know a lot about gardening and I also gardened at home for my mother. We grew whatever we needed to eat.

When the war broke out I was a gardening Chauffeur. I begin driving in the mid 1930s, for Major Piggott at the Rectory, Bletsoe. Mrs Piggott was Chairlady of the Directors of Mansfield Shoe Company in Northampton. I had been working for her, and her husband asked if I would like to be chauffeur, as the previous one had left. I willingly agreed and was sent on a "refresher course", though I had no experience of driving at that time and had never received tuition. There weren't many cars on the road in those days. I had six one-hourly lessons with a local instructor, which included instruction in how to start and stop the car, where to put the oil and water in, things like that. There was so little traffic on the road you couldn't get it wrong. My employers paid for my tuition and then gave me permission to take the car out at any time to practice, and this I did, – drove for miles.

You could go for miles then without seeing another car. After a few weeks, as I recall, I felt quite confident and began my chauffeuring duties. There were two cars, an Alvis 17, 1930 and an Austin saloon. The Alvis's accelerator was in the middle, so it was a terrifying experience switching from one car to the other and trying to remember the pedal sequences. I have only driven one car like it since, which was a Ford, just after the war. They felt exactly the same to handle.

For my job as chauffeur, I was supplied with all the clothes required, shoes, socks, white shirts, black tie, double breasted, navy blue suit, blue mackintosh, kid gloves and peak cap. I always opened the doors, which was really a matter of courtesy, just good manners. I was always careful not to walk in front of the car if anyone was in it.

Some of the roads were much wider than now, but the country roads were very different, and unmade. Occasionally Mrs Piggott drove herself, but if she was going to be late home at night I took her, and always met her at the station. I used to take her daughter to the meeting of the hounds. It was much more enjoyable than gardening, but there was gardening to do, as chauffeuring wasn't a full-time job. One of my responsibilities was to keep the car clean, – it was essential to keep it clean and tidy, inside and out. I never had a break-down, and only once can I remember seeing another Alvis. I never saw any others like it. When it snowed there was no anti-freeze, and there were no heaters. There was a bonnet over the radiator for warming up in the winter time. There was no salt on the road, and we had to carry chains and fit them to the back wheels, to cut through the snow. It was an awful job fitting them and as soon as the snow went they had to come off or they would tear the tyres to pieces.

I don't remember seeing any rust on the cars then, they were better made than they are today. The Alvis was the master's car. I can still remember the first ever car in Thurleigh, – the first telephone too.

This was the best job I ever had, – very nice people. They were wealthy people but they treated you as a human being.

Driving tests started in 1935 but I had my licence before then, of course. I did have a test in the army, and one for the Ministry of Defence.

My first car was a Triumph, a Pillarless, four-door model. I had never seen one like it before, nor have I since.'

JOHN 'JACK' THORNE

A Housemaid

'To be a domestic servant was a highly desirable form of employment because it guaranteed that a person could eat regularly, have a clean comfortable bed to sleep in and by observing the actions of those around you, learn how to "Dress correctly", "Speak correctly", "Table etiquette", "Manners", which, really means "How to live a good clean life". Young people of the nineteenth century could never hope to live so well in what was, by today's standards, homes that were little more than hovels and where the weekly income was barely adequate to feed the family. The girls of most poor families were sent into "Service" as soon as they left school which then permitted the rest of the family to eat more.

A Housemaid's Day

0630   *Rise, wash and dress (including large white apron), clean drawing room, Master's study and Lady's den, clean out fire places, polish, relay fires then awaken the "Family". Prepare hot water for baths. After "Family" had gone down to breakfast, run out water and clean baths, make beds and tidy bedrooms. Fill coalscuttle.*

0830   *Have breakfast in servants' hall.*

0900   *Collect oil lamps from downstairs rooms and candlesticks from bedrooms, clean and refill.*

1200   *Have lunch then dress in black dress with frilly white cap, white apron, stiff collar and cuffs, black stockings and shoes.*
              During the afternoon repair household linen and also do the "special weekly work" according to the day of the week.

1600   *Have tea in servants' hall.*

1900   *Take hot water to bedrooms, "Family" would then wash, dress for dinner and go down to a seven course meal.*

1945   *Turn down beds, fill hotwater bottle, set candlestick on bedside tables but, if there was a guest for dinner, housemaid helped wait on table to assist parlour-maid.*

2100   *Help parlour-maid to wash silver in the parlour-maid's pantry.*

2200   *Have supper in kitchen then go to bed.*

Special Weekly Work

Monday   *Clean drawing room and spare bedroom alternately, collect and count laundry.*

Tuesday   *Clean two bedrooms.*

Wednesday *Clean servants' bedrooms and housemaid's pantry.*

Thursday   *Clean bathroom, lavatory and staircase.*

Friday   *Clean library and morning room.*

Saturday   *Put away linen from washing and make things generally tidy ready for Sunday.'*

H S BROWN

'I was a housemaid at Hawne School [Haynes], which opened in December 1929. Before that it was used as a private house. It was originally the home of Lord and Lady Thynne who were local landowners.

Miss Townsend and Miss Chapman started the school, and when about a dozen or so of us went down for a job, we were surprised to see these two women whose heels were worn and who were not dressed up as we expected them to be.

We had to live in at the school. We used to have to get on our hands and knees and polish the place. We cleaned the main staircase and the hall, did the headmistress's rooms, the washing up and so on. I was responsible for cleaning the dormatories, which were in the attics. Mrs Thompson, the parlour maid, came in 1930. It was her job to wait on tables.

There was no life at Hawne School and nothing to do. If we went out to a dance we had to be back at a certain time. The food was good though. Mrs Covington was the cook at that time. My mother was in service all her life, and she seemed to like the job, but I personally like to work in a place where you

Hawne School, originally the home of Lord Thynne, later to become Clarendon School until 1991.
Photo: courtesy The Headmistress, Miss J Howell.

can have a laugh, where there is a bit of life. One night when I got back from a dance, they were doing fire drill and I had to join in, and this was my night off! On Sundays all the children were sent to church, and this took up three parts of the church. Confirmations were done at the church once a year. We're very proud of our church: do you know, part of the gold cloth used in Queen Victoria's coronation robes is one of our treasured possessions.'

BEATRICE 'MAY' WEBB

The Cook's Daughter

'My mother was a professional cook, and she came from Denton, Grantham (nr. Barraby), Lincolnshire. She had eight children, and my father died in 1906 when I was two. He died of double pneumonia. He had been a luggage carrier on the railway, a carrier for the ladies. I had to go with my mother

Marjorie's mother, Elizabeth, with (left to right) four of her children, Walter, Dora, Marjorie and May.

as she moved from one country place to another, one big house to another, as a professional cook. I do remember that she made lovely cakes.

My mother's sister (Fanny Sibthorpe) took my two sisters in and gave them a good education, but they didn't want me. My

Marjorie's parent's wedding in the 1890s.

Marjorie Glenford's
maternal grandparents
at their cottage in
Denton, Grantham,
near Barraby.

Aunt Fanny
(Mrs Sibthorpe),
Marjorie Glenford's
mother's sister.

William Sibthorpe, Marjorie's uncle,
a one-time sergeant major.

uncle (William Sibthorpe) was a sergeant major in the army and he was transferred to Bedford and that's how I came to be here. I lived with him and the old aunt at times, when my mother couldn't have me living with her at the houses where she worked. My uncle and aunt brought me up from eleven, and I went to Goldington Road School.

Marjorie (right) aged seven, with cousin May, with whom she lived at one time.

One of my aunts that I stayed with had a little farmhouse in the country, and they had all sorts of animals. My cousin May and I went into the barn and there was a see-saw there and we thought we would have a game. She let me down quickly, and I broke my arm. I had to go through ploughed fields to see the doctor with it broken. I was in pain with it, all night. I was seven then. This was the one experience of play which I remember. It was a job to get to the hospital because they had no transport then: we went in a horse and cart and my poor arm did hurt. Students did it and didn't set it properly. It is still wrong. They had to conjour up things in the medical line then. It was not like it is now. This was at Grantham Hospital in Lincolnshire.

When I got to the age of eleven or so I had to go back to this old aunt, but unlike my sisters, I had to go to the elementary school. I went into service at the age of fourteen. My mother died when I was sixteen: I was working at Dame Alice School [Bedford] House then, but was not with my mother.

I had little time for play as a child, it was all work. I was passed from one old aunt to another old aunt because my

Servants from the Big House. Believed to be Marjorie's mother and mother's sister (housemaid and lady's maid), and Marjorie's brother, Walter, the boot boy.

mother was left with four children and I couldn't always be with her at work. My old Aunt Fanny was very strict but I do not regret it because I think it has brought me out.

When I lived with my mother in the big house I had to work too, making beds, laying tables, doing vegetables, helping mother to get dinners at night, helping her to prepare. Once we went into a big house, mother and I, and there was a gentleman there I had to call "Sir". He had a little room where he kept private things and he had a little box with the letters in, rubbish. I cleaned his room out every morning. One morning at the bottom of the box I found 6d. I told him and he said "You can keep it Marjorie, for being an honest girl". After that there was money left all over the place because he knew he could trust me.

I started work when I was about fourteen, like a sort of children's maid. The children I had charge of were four and five year olds. I looked after them and took them out daily and I earned half a crown a week and then it went up to five shillings. This was when I got a job on my own. When I worked in service at Dame Alice Schoolhouse in Bedford there was a French lady and a girl who couldn't speak English and her mother asked me to teach her. I didn't know if I had the brains to do it! She was very pleased that I did teach her. She asked me to go to Belgium with her. I didn't but I wish now that I had. The girl was about seven or eight when I first knew her. I think her mother was a teacher at the school, very well-to-do people. Her husband was a very nice man too.

I quite enjoyed life with my mother. If she had a place in service where they couldn't take children then I went to my aunt. I was in Nottingham when I was five and started school there. I went to about eleven different schools. I didn't learn much but I have learned a lot since. Once of my sisters won a scholarship for Bishop's Stortford and one went to Dame Alice. My brother Walter never married. he has been a butler and has waited on royalty. He has been all his working life at Irnham Hall, Irnham, near Grantham and Irnham Hall is still owned by the same people – "Sir Simon". There are now one or two cleaners at the mansion and hall, and if they have a party and want the silver cleaned, he still does it for them.'

MARJORIE GLENFORD

Majorie's aunts, with whom she lived on occasions.

THE FARM

THE FARM

Introduction

Even up to the time of the second world war, many rural dwellers worked on the land at intervals, though not necessarily as a full-time occupation. It was common, for instance, for a man to work in the brickyards through the winter and do seasonal work at other times of the year, helping with hay cutting, corn harvesting and crop picking. People also went to Lincolnshire and Mill Hill to cut hay crops by hand, working in teams, and living locally until the task was completed. The leader of the gang, the man at the front, was known as the lord. This leader had his scythe set at a lesser width than the others so he could work at a quicker pace, since he made a lesser swath. This is thought to be the origin of the phrase 'drunk as a lord', as the lord got the beer from the farmer for the refreshment of the gang!

In areas of Bedfordshire there were various crops to be picked, – peas, potatoes, brussels and so on. Stone picking was also done to clear the ground, so as to minimise damage to equipment. Few are willing to hand-pick crops nowadays, other than travellers, who return annually for the sole purpose of crop-picking.

Since there are no subsidies for the growing of vegetables many farmers are diversifying and fertile land is sadly being used for industrial units and housing developments.

In earlier days the farmhouse and farm buildings were the nerve centre of the farming community. Large imposing buildings, often approached by a long driveway and set in the middle of the fields and farmland which formed a part of the farm. The cowsheds, the piggery, the granary, the stables, the dairy, the barns, the courtyard, the farmworkers' cottages, – an industrial unit engineered by nature, harnessed and fashioned by human hand, driven by horse-power and by manual labour.

The farmhouse kitchen, in particular, holds a nostalgia for many, and – for those of us fortunate enough to be able to visit such places – the farmhouse kitchen at Beamish Open Air Museum in the north of England provides an unforgettable experience of traditional farmhouse life. The most attractive feature of the enormous kitchen is a roaring fire blazing heat from a huge black-leaded range, complete with water tank and oven. Brass door knobs, meat hooks hanging from racks, stands, skillets, pots and pans, kettles, all the paraphernalia associated with cooking on an open range. The warmth, the smell and sound of burning coals and wood, the dimly-lit room with hanging oil-lamps, the stone-flagged floor, rag rugs, the feel of touch-smoothed old wooden settles and chairs, the smoke-tarnished ceiling, beams supporting clothes airers and racks for drying oat cakes and the like. Large oak dresser displaying enormous serving dishes and plates, racks of cast-iron pots and pans, copper skillets, brass ornaments and trimmings on the grate, the smell of home-made bread, stews, pies! One cannot begin to understand the sensuality, the sheer joy of the experience of the living farmhouse kitchen.

From 4.30am each morning there was activity at the farmhouse, often beginning with hand-milking of the dairy herd. Was the farmhouse a comfortable place in which to live? The working day on the farm was a long day, and animals needed tending seven days a week. For the farmer and his sons, the farmhouse was essentially a place to eat and to sleep. Many farms had no piped water, and this meant that the animals had to be watered by hand, with buckets of water taken from a pump or (as on one village farm) from a moat containing spring water. Watering dairy herds, horses and other animals once bedded down for the night, was a time-consuming and arduous task for men tired from a long day's toil. For the farmer's wife, daughters and maids, life centred more on the farmhouse, but was equally as demanding.

Girls in service on the farm, who lived in and worked as maids at the farmhouse were paid around £18 a year, fed and accommodated and given a print dress for working in and a black dress for the afternoons. Daily domestic labour was always available.

'On a Monday mother had an old girl come in to do her washing, and she was paid 1/- for this, – 1/- to walk across two fields to wash, and then to come back on Tuesday and do the ironing for another shilling. This was Mrs Luck, and she lived opposite the old school: this was when we farmed at Wood Farm, Wootton. In those days [seventy years ago] labour was plentiful and it was cheap. When I started work on my father's farm at thirteen, I was paid ten shillings a week. I had to clothe myself out of that. Father employed a Horsekeeper, named Brightman, and a fellow called Ayres, who was the Cowman. They had 35/- a week. Ordinary men [farm workers] had 25/- and the ploughboy had 12/-.

Of all the farmworkers and their children you never saw them in ragged clothes. They were always dressed respectably because their wives were managers.

My mother used to do most, if not all of the cooking on the kitchen range. She had help to do the washing in the wooden tub and in putting things through the mangle. Mother only had one live-in maid. The maids lived in the kitchen and we lived in the dining room. The live-in maid worked as our waitress at mealtimes, and we'd ring the bell for service. They fed in the kitchen. When I was about nine [1918] we had a maid, aged about twenty-five, called Florrie. Once morning my mother called her down but she didn't come so mother *went up to her room and found she had had a baby in the night! We didn't know she was pregnant. She had delivered it herself and put it in the bottom drawer of the chest of drawers. She was put in a home after that, with the child – as far as I know – and mother got a new maid. There was a Domestic Agency in Bromham Road, Bedford, and they could arrange domestic help. Some maids were asking for £25 a year, but mother couldn't afford more than £18, but that included board and lodging, a print dress to work in and a black dress for afternoons.*

Mother kept poultry and made and sold butter as well as eggs. This was her side-line. She always had plenty to do, even with domestic help. There was the cooking, cleaning, laundry, mending and darning, rag mat making, and she enjoyed reading occasionally.

Farmhouse food was wholesome and delicious. Apple pies, rabbit pies. Food cooked on the range was lovely, no comparison with the pastry cooked in today's ovens. Mother often did Bedfordshire Clangers, and they could be eaten hot or cold. She made them to be eaten at home. Then she'd make Swimmers (dumplins) which she cooked with the Bedfordshire Clangers. The Swimmers were eaten hot, with butter and sugar. You always made dumplins, to eke out your meat. Jugged hare and redcurrant jelly was wonderful. That was cooked in an earthenware pot, stewed with a shin of beef. The hare was cut into joints before cooking, and onion was added for flavouring. We'd eat that with potatoes and greens. Rabbit pies! The joints were put into a pie dish, and pastry laid on top. You could put pickled pork or hardboiled egg in with it. Delicious! Pickled pork is belly pork, salted for about a week and boiled. It's eaten cold the next day or can then be put into your rabbit pie. I don't remember mother doing wine-making, but when she died we found a bottle of home-made elderberry liqueur which she'd made and that was dated 1898.

Food was plentiful: you cut your pattern according to your cloth, so to speak. Many farm workers were self-supporting as

A typical farmhouse kitchen.

regards vegetables and some had allotments. Most had poultry and pigs. We were infested with rabbits and were glad for people to catch them. Wild wood pigeons we were smothered with too, but pigeon is the most indigestable of meats and not many people ate it. Nobody went hungry in those days.

FRED FROSSELL

The Farmer

Asked, with his eightieth birthday fast approaching, whether he was making plans for retirement, Fred Frossell looked genuinely surprised and perplexed: 'but what would I do if I retired?'

Fred's working day begins at 6.30am, with breaks for breakfast and lunch. At 3.35pm after a break for a cup of tea, proceedings in the Frossell household come to an abrupt halt and Fred dashes off to work again. His working day is well-ordered, and consists of a rigid routine with everything running like clock-work. His modest home is spotlessly clean, tidy and organised, as is his farm. He is incredibly agile of mind and body, a dedicated man who knows his business and has the energy and determination to ensure the success of his farming operation.

Fred's son is moderately progressive in farming matters. on the subject of beagling he observed, somewhat derisively, 'are they hunting hares or are they exercising their dogs?' Father corrects him – 'hounds!' On shooting: 'this is the farmer's sport: we invite our friends over for shoots and they invite us. Yes, shooting parties are usually male, but not always. We shoot grouse and pheasants.' On the subject of farm horses, asked whether he would use horses on the farm, he was negative, and even sceptical about their usefulness in cities such as London. He doubted that they are more economic than lorries, used as drays. Regarding their suitability for working on soils where mechanised vehicles have proven damaging, he thought this might apply in other parts of the country such as Norfolk but not in this area. He shows no sign of nostalgia for the days of the farm horse.

The Frossell family's success in surviving the agricultural depression and succeeding in an industry where many have failed, says much for the enterprise, dedication and deter-mination of this family, through several generations. Fred expressed concern about the future, since his only grandson displays less interest and enthusiasm for farming – or certainly for arable farming – than Fred considers necessary to ensure the survival of this family concern. He did say, however, with some pride, that his grand-daughter is shortly to marry and that she is marrying into a farming family.

'I was born in 1909 at Wood Farm, Wootton Green. Wood Farm belonged to Sir Phillip Payne, and my father was a tenant-farmer there for sixteen years. We later moved to Houghton Conquest to farm, and then my father found a farm he wanted to buy and we moved to Wick End Farm in Stagsden, where we remained for sixty-six years.

A recent photgraph of Wick End Farm. Photo: courtesy Councillor Tucker.

As far as I am aware, our family association with farming goes back to the time when my father farmed in Manitoba, Canada, for a period of about ten years. His brother died there, in Brandon. It was hard out there and the weather could be extremely cold. Before his migration to Canada, I think my grandfather, Charles Frossell, was a baker at Biddenham. From this interest with farming in Canada, our whole family became involved. Both of my brothers farmed: Ernest, the eldest, and Jim, my youngest brother. Jim last farmed at Salford near Cranfield, before retiring. I have a cousin at Wood End, who was one of Ernest's children. Jim farmed Kempston Bury, Wood End Farm, where they now live, and West End Farm, Kempston. I feel that my father would have returned to Canada after we left Wootton Green, but we felt that mother couldn't withstand the hardship. We were quite big farmers in the county: my present acreage is approximately eight hundred.

My brothers and I went to Bedford Modern School in Harpur Street, Bedford. I was not taught much that was relevant to farming: the school was not so much interested in agriculture as it was in the professions and sport. In those days there weren't many jobs for young people locally: there was more employment in agriculture and farming and I knew and my father knew, that I would leave school and work on the farm. I left school at thirteen. My father was farming at Wick End Farm and my eldest brother was working for him. Seven people worked on the farm at that time, and all the milking was done by hand, starting at 4.30 in the morning. We had about forty cows. I used to get up and milk four cows every morning before going to school, and loved doing it.

Wick End was half arable, half grass. Everything was done by horses and hand work. There were three of us and we employed three people – the horsekeeper, the cowman and the ploughboy and two odd-job men who would do hedging and ditching, which was all done by hand in those days. Sometimes these men would bring in some of their children to help. Harvesting was all done by hand too. The men came from the villages to help.

Wick End Farm, Stagsden, in earlier times, photographed from the rear. Photo: courtesy Mr H Welch.

We started milking at 4.30am and the milk had to be at Spring Road, Kempston by 7.00am, taken in by the pony and float to the dairy. The dairyman employed roundsmen who went out with the trucks and it was all sold out of cans with a pint or half-pint measure. This was pure milk, just as milked, raw and straight from the cow. It never poisoned anybody. In the winter the dairymen paid eighteen pence a gallon and in the summertime a shilling, because when the cows were out to grass their yields went up – "the flush" it was called. What the dairymen couldn't take, we put through a separator – there were always surpluses in the summer – to get the cream out and from this cream, butter was made, on the farm. This was put in a big barrel with a handle at a certain temperature and we turned the barrel round until the butter came. If you went too fast the cream would "go to sleep" as we said. The butter came all at once; there was glass in the barrel and you could see when it cleared that the butter was ready. The buttermilk which was left was fed to the pigs. Our grocer took this fresh farm butter. He was an old family grocer who lived at Kempston. We sold him eggs from the poultry, and surplus butter which we'd made from the flush of milk.

My mother knew one of the more influential members of the Bunyan Meeting (Braggins) and when the Bunyan Farm came up for letting, my wife and I got it. We rented it for a few years and then eventually we were able to buy it. We've been here ever since. My wife was from Sherrington, Bucks., and hers was a farming family too. My brother, mother and father continued to farm at Wick End, until my father was thrown off a cart and broke his back. My mother and brother carried on farming until she died, and then my brothers and I split the farm up between us. I've bought quite a lot of the land back off my eldest brother since then.

Our farming interests have developed over the years. I bought Roundhill Farm, a diary farm in Stagsden, from Mr Marvin, then Dropshort Farm from Mr Rose, and four years ago I bought Wood Farm in Newton Blossomville. My sons and I still farm these individually. We increased our land as agriculture became more mechanised and we could cope with the work. My sons have worked on my farm ever since they left school. They went to Rushmore School. They never had any desire to do anything else other than farming.

We have always been careful to select those farms which were conveniently located so as to be economic of time, but one farm is about four and a half miles away, at Newton Blossomville. However, there are buildings with it and we are able to store a certain amount of machinery there. We bring all the corn back here at harvest time. We put rape seed there in three fifty-ton bins – you can't mix this with corn. This has been grown for about ten or fifteen years. That far back there were only about two people who grew it locally but they found other uses for it – oil, etc. – and so nearly every farmer came to grow it. It was an early crop and you could get it off the land before the corn. It is made into cooking oil, and margarine. After it is crushed the solid waste is used in cattle feed. The residue is rich and ideal for cattle feed.

Joy riders at the Shuttleworth Open Day 1990, learning about horse power!

In years gone by village life was woven around agriculture. We were infested with children at harvest time, the field was full of children coming to help. Scores of women folk walked from Wootton to glean. They picked up the gleanings that came out of the sheaths, put them in a bag and gleaned enough to keep them in the winter time in flour. It was thrashed when the machine came to the village, and it then went to Kempston Mill to be ground into flour. The road runs parallel with Water Lane, it was called Mr Clover's mill. It was ground into flour. Directly we cleared a field we left a shock in the middle to show they could not glean until it was finished with. They picked up bags of it. There was no waste.

People were just as happy in those olden times. Nobody had got much money and there weren't things to do as there are today, no television and so on, but they were just as happy. The children were always tidy. The women knitted and darned and made rag rugs.

We grew mangolds and swedes for cattle feed. These had to be pulled, carted, pitted (strawed for the winter) and the cattle had to be fed. All of this feed came from the farm, mangolds, worzels, chaff. Today this is bought in in cubes containing the necessary oil and fibre. Think how much labour that saves! All the straw was taken into the rick yard in the sheaths, thrashed and used for litter and feed for the cattle but nowadays it is burnt.

When we have finished combining, we want to start ploughing it for the next crop. You haven't got time for collecting up and bailing straw for condensing and domestic burning, which they are now talking about doing.

We have employed quite a lot of people over the years. People would come and go, moving from one farm to another. We have had land girls working for us at different times and one or two patients from Bromham Hospital, who lived in. They were paid so much and the hospital was paid so much. During the war time there were a lot of Italian and German prisoners, three or four each day. I cannot remember any such thing as "payment in kind": I think this must have been before my time and perhaps before my father's time. We have never dealt in farm workers' cottages either. One chap was with us for fifty-seven years, Sid Summerlin, – and the Welch family, they were there with us for a long time, – he was cowman. I believe Mr Welch then worked for the Newman farmers in Stagsden, as horsekeeper.

The men took so much interest in their job and were proud of it. If the cows looked well and were clean it was their pride. They had nothing but this to do, except a day out at the Bedford Show where they proudly showed the animals which they had bred and cared for. These people always kept a few chickens in a run and a pig at the bottom of the garden, which was fattened and slaughtered, but it was the farm animals which they took a pride in.

I remember the Corn Exchange in Bedford, where merchants used to have their stalls and farmers brought in the samples of grain in little bags to try and sell, – wheat, barley, clover seed. There were quite a few merchants there buying. It was a big day and after the cattle market finished on Saturdays, they went to the Corn Exchange to sell their corn. Dudeney & Johnson's was a popular restaurant with the farming community who would meet there on Saturday for lunch after market. This was in the High Street on the same side as Debenhams, between the fruit market and Harpur Street. Farmers would leave their horses at the George pub in the High Street, whilst at market.'

FREDERICK FROSSELL

A Farmer's Daughter

'My father was a tenant farmer and my brothers all worked on the farm. There was only the traditional type of occupation available in the village. Many women made pillow lace and walked into town to sell it to Braggins. Women also did

Eveline Stanton, aged 24.

gleaning at harvesting time, but the majority of women worked in the home. I was interest in nursing, but having suffered with the fever which spread during the war, I hadn't the necessary strength for this. I had been attended by a very good doctor from Barford, who called almost every day to treat me, and people in the village were kind enough to come and sit with me, although I later had a nurse. I was more fortunate than many people, as my father was able to pay for medical fees. As I recovered from my illness my doctor suggested that I should take up poultry farming, as father had plenty of land, and this I did.

Eggs were collected each week by someone from St. Neots, and with the help of my brothers and a man we employed to clean out the hens, I developed the poultry farm. As for the chickens, some we ate and some we sold at the market. I also kept ducks. My brothers had the job of wringing necks! Father kept a lot of pigs, and these used to be slaughtered by someone in the village. With no fridges, meat had to be salted for

Abbey Farm near Elstow. Farmhands at work stacking and rick-making. Photo: messrs Fox Photos Ltd.

Abbey Farm. Photo: Messrs Fox Photos Ltd.

Harvesting at Elstow. Photo: Messrs Fox Photos Ltd.

preservation, and it could then be kept for months. I think sugar and treacle were also used in the preserving process. The hams were lovely then, not like today. Mother cooked lovely meals, big joints, Yorkshire pudding, trifles, milk puddings, bread pudding, and always plenty of vegetables which father grew. She also made her own butter, using a barrel and patting it up.

When my father gave up farming at Rectory Farm, my brother and I took on Abbey Farm, Elstow. This was along Ampthill Road. I ran the home and he farmed, and when he retired, we moved to Meppersham and bought a property with fields attached, but we didn't farm. It was a poor village then but has since been built up. After his death I moved again, to be nearer to my sister who lived at Little Staughton, but in our family of eight children, I am now the sole survivor.'

EVELINE STANTON

The Farm House

'*After leaving school I nursed my mother for a time as she was ill and then went into service with Mrs Horrell, at Strawberry Hill Farm. My working day began at 7.15am and ended at 5.30pm, and on Saturday 7.15am–1.30pm and Sunday 8.00am–1.30pm. I trimmed the oil lamps, cleaned the wicks, scrubbed the floor, washed the hens' eggs, cleaned the glasses, did the ironing and carried the water upstairs for the bedrooms. They all had wash stands, father, mother and their two daughters, and guests. I also did the fires, but they only had fires in the bedrooms if anyone was ill. They were a spartan lot! There were chamber pots to be emptied and wash bowls to be emptied and cleaned. We had separate days for different jobs. Monday was washing, and Monday afternoon ironing, but there was a pulley for drying the washing if the weather was bad, and the ironing was left until Tuesday. Tuesday was normally bedroom day, when they were done well. Other days the beds were just made but the room wasn't cleaned. Wednesdays was drawing room day. Friday was dining room and Saturday was scrubbing day – breadboards, rolling pins, pastry boards, kitchen tables and so on, and everything was stood out in the sun. Of the five shillings a week which I was paid, I banked 2/6d, spent one shilling on the bus, 9d on the pictures, 3d on sweets and had 3d in my pocket. I was given my breakfast, lunch and supper.*

The mistress did the cooking herself and there were odd job men, like the cowman, who lit the copper each day in the wash-house for sterilising all the milk churns. All the utensils had to be sterilized, and this was our source of hot water. Each afternoon he would bring in a bucket of milk and in the pantry there were two large flat pans where it stood until morning, when the cream was taken off the top and butter made, once a week. That was made in the churn. In the farmhouses you had to pump water up, as there was a pump in the back scullery. Pumping filled the tank upstairs so water was available by tap from the tank.

I had to top up the lamps with paraffin. On one occasion soon after I started, I was told to put paraffin on the fire if it went down. I thought I had let the copper fire out, and opened the fireplace and threw some on it and it immediately blew back and burnt my eyebrows and scorched my hair.

It was a very varied life.'

WINIFRED ALLAN

The Cowman

'I worked on the farm for the first seven years after leaving school, starting at 6.00am and finishing 5.00pm, and for ten shillings a week. I was allowed half an hour for breakfast, and one hour for dinner.

When I started, I used to drive the plough, helping my father, and also did odd jobs hedging and ditching and general farm work. When my brother started working on the farm I was given two horses to manage my own ploughing, with my own team. My father used to get the horses in in the morning, fed and ready for me to leave with them at 6 o'clock. We worked until 2.00pm and then my father fed and cleaned them. 2.00–3.00pm was dinner-time and then there were odd jobs to be done such as getting coal and wood for the farm house, fencing and such like.

At one time my father looked after thirty shire horses, and he had the first double farrow plough that was turned out in Bedford at the Brittania Iron Works, established in 1859 by John Howard's sons James and Frederick, to produce agricultural implements. We won first prize that first year in the agricultural show. The certificate he was awarded is still a prized family possession.

When I was twenty-one, I left the farm and went onto the railway, as this paid an extra ten shillings a week, although I had to bike seven miles each way to get it. I was a plate layer – a ganger – through Stewartby Brick Works, for five years. I had six men working under me, and our job was to maintain the lines.

After my marriage I returned to work on the farm and moved back to Kempston Wood End, then to Turvey, where I got a tied cottage near Turvey Grove Farm, which is now a built-up area.

I was cowman on the farm for thirty years altogether. The cowman does the calving, records how much each cow yields, takes care of the registration of the cows, of pedigrees. All the milking was done by machine at that time, after the second world war, and the milk had to be cooled to a certain temperature and then used to be collected and brought into Bedford to the dairies, – to Biddenham Dairies.

I'm happy with what I've done in the past, and with my work on the farm. I don't feel that I have missed any opportunities in life.'

HERBERT WELCH

The Horsekeeper

Until well into the twentieth century the horse provided the power required on the farm, and care of the horses – Shire horses generally – was entrusted to the Horsekeeper. The Horsekeeper was one of the key workers on the farm, holding a position of some considerable importance among farm workers.

A Typical Horsekeeper's Day

0430	*Rise, have cup of tea.*
0500	*Arrive at farm. Feed, water and clean horses.*
0600	*Go home to breakfast.*
0645	*Return to farm. Harness horses ready for day's work according to type of work to be done that day.*
0715	*Take two or three of the horses and proceed to plough or cultivate land. Other farm hands would take the remaining horses for other work.*
1000	*Stop work for half hour's tea break.*
1030	*Resume work as before.*
1300	*Stop for sandwich and a cup of tea.*
1315	*Resume work as before.*

1500	*Disconnect farm equipment from the horses and return to farm via some convenient pond where the horses' hooves would be washed.* *It was expected that by this time the team would have ploughed or cultivated an acre or acre and one rood dependent on the furrow required by the farmer.*
1515	*Unharness horses, water and feed them, then rub them down with straw before putting them into the stables.*
1545	*Go home to dinner.*
1615	*Return to farm. Take horses out of stables for a drink whilst stable lad cleaned out the stalls. Whilst horses drinking prepare their evening meal. Return horses to stables and give them a thorough clean which, it should be noted, was extremely hard work. During the winter the horses were bedded down with straw but in the summer they were turned out into a meadow.*
1715	*Return home for tea.*

Ploughing at Barton Hills. 'Approached by a long cutting . . . a vista of rural beauty opens out to the visitor. Its hills and springs are a source of attraction to many tourists.'
Luton and Neighbourhood Illustrated, publisher T G Hobbs.

On Sundays he would go to the farm at 0700 to clean and feed horses and he would repeat that at 1530.

The horses were considered as friends and were loved by all who tended them. A ploughman would talk to his team of horses all day long and they would listen to him intently.'

H S BROWN

On many farms the horsekeeper, who would be up and about soon after five o'clock, was on duty shortly after this time and he would feed, then gear and harness the horses. The team of three horses would leave the farm between seven and eight o'clock to trek to the field where the work of the day was to be done. A 'tommy bag' containing the men's food would be taken. Around a couple of hours' work would be done before a break for breakfast during which the horses would be given a nosebag. Ploughing would then continue until approximately 2.00pm. Then the team would be unharnessed and taken home. After going home to their dinner, the horsekeeper and ploughboy would return to groom the horses and clean out the stables. Also to clean the harness and the horse brasses. These are items very much in demand today.

'A recognised day of ploughing would cover about one acre of land, and this meant the men and horses walking a distance of about eleven miles. I sometimes visit the field where I first did some of this work, and I ruminate on the difference nowadays when the same acreage is probably covered by tractor in about an hour. Even the development of tractors has progressed considerably. It is now necessary by law for all new tractors to be fitted with cabs. This covers a safety aspect and also means that ploughing continues in wet weather.'

WALTER 'REG' PARROTT

The Farm Worker

'My father was a farm worker and he worked at various farms around Stagsden. When I left school there wasn't much work, things were very slack. There was no full-time work locally at any rate. I'd worked on a local farm which belonged to the Frossells and when the farmer died the farm was split up between the farmer's sons. The farmhouse is now occupied by Councillor Tucker. One of the farmer's sons lives in Stagsden and still farms in the area.

Stagsden used to be all Crown land, and it was sold in about 1920 and the farmers 'ad the opportunity to buy their own farms. Jack Wright bought the farm at Wick End, and then sold it to the Frossells.

There was no apprenticeship – you learned it yourself. I continued to work on the farm on Saturdays, and after three years I was offered full-time work there. There was plenty o' variety in farm work, ploughing and drilling, with a team o' four 'orses, then 'arrowing, working with a team o' three 'orses. The 'arrow covers the corn, and after 'arrowing, it's rolled, in the springtime. Two 'orses would draw a single plough, and

The last load! From Year Book & Directory for 1913.
Photo: courtesy Dunstable Gazette.

four a double plough, which was twice as wide. You'd be lucky to plough an acre a day with a single plough, but it could be done with a good team of 'orses. To do this the ploughman or ploughboy would walk a distance of eleven miles. At 'arvest time the binder was pulled by 'orses – before the days of tractors. The binder cuts it and throws it out in sheaths. You'd go be'ind it and stand the shocks of corn, and when they were dry they were carted and stacked in the Dutch barns.

There were 'edges to be trimmed and fencing to be checked, every year. Drainage ditches were cleared out every year too. 'Edge laying paid one shilling per chain, that's twenty-two yards: piece rate that was. 'Edge laying is interweaving, and we 'ad to use a chopper to do this, called a "bill". The 'edge 'ad to be laid, staked, and bound along the top to keep it down. This should end up about shoulder 'eight and would last for several years. It 'ad to be done to keep the animals in. Barbed wire was put alongside the 'edge until it became established, to keep the animals from rubbing against it. 'Edge trimming was done to keep it down to size.

There was a local blacksmith in Stagsden by the name o' Austin Summerlin, who did repairs and shoed the 'orses – no relation o'mine. Mr Bazeley was the village wheelwright and undertaker, and the baker lived next to 'im. The baker also ran a shop and the Post Office. There was a watchmaker and mender, Joel Jackson, and 'e also kept bees. George Wallinger was the local carrier. I can't remember there being a village butcher or doctor. In fact when the land was owned by the Crown, several properties were built in Bedford Road which were purpose-built 'omes and shops and one of these I am told, was a butcher's. William Odell was shopkeeper and pork butcher at one time. During the time of Crown ownership, twenty pole plots were chopped down every year from the Angus and Astin Woods to be sold for firewood. This was just clearance of undergrowth, part o' the estate management. Nearly all the land in this parish was purchased by the Crown in 1873, 3,386 acres.

I've 'elped the cowman, 'orseman and shepherd on the farm. These were the 'ead Men. There were generally ten or twelve men employed on a farm. I 'elped with feeding and watering the animals too. If they needed attention, a vet came over from Kempston.

It used to be illegal to poach and snare animals, but I 'ave known it done. I used to beat for the farmer when they were shooting pheasants and 'ares. Most villagers kept pigs, and one man in the village used to go around the village slaughtering the pigs which were then scolded and the 'airs scraped off. They'd be scolded, salted and 'ung. There were deer locally but these weren't killed.

I retired at sixty-seven, but I 'ave done odd jobs 'ere and there since. I've enjoyed life and 'ad some good times. I used to walk miles, to Wick End and back every day to work, and to Bedford and back on Sunday nights to go to the pictures, when I was a lad. It was one and 'alf miles to school from our 'ome at the Toll 'ouse (just before the turn to the Northampton Road, along Bromham). When we lived there my father worked at Bromham 'ouse which is now the 'ospital. W H Allen owned it, and the Iron Works in Bedford. Allens were also farmers and my father farmed for them.

Sid Summerlin, farmworker, at work in Stagsden.

I've only 'ad the doctor once in my life, when I fractured my wrist 'edging and was off work for three months. During that time I was paid from the Sick Club, the National United Order of Tree Gardeners Friendly Society. I've been in good 'ealth all my life and I've smoked all my life. I used to smoke old man's beard – the stem of it – when I was at school.'

SIDNEY SUMMERLIN

'I worked on the farm with my dad when I left school, at thirteen, and I continued to be a farm worker until I was fifty-six, and then after operations on both knees, I was not able to return to farming.

My father was horse keeper. At one time during my working life, the farm itself changed hands. From March of that year until September, everything was very quiet, until the sale was completed. During this time my father went to work for someone else and I then took over my parents' tied cottage, and married. After eight years I moved to Wick End Farm and worked there for twenty-seven years. My father died at the age of eighty and my mother at eighty-seven.

On the farm, money was always scarce. After I retired a friend of mine remarked that I was no better off than when I started, but my answer to that was that I had made a living from farming and had been able to bring up a family on the proceeds. I'd enjoyed working with horses: I never had any mechanical knowledge, and have never worked with tractors. For the last twenty-seven years on the farm I was milking cows and looking after cattle. I have no interest in present-day farming, mechanisation, crop spraying and the like.

The Bedfordshire Agricultural Society was formed in 1801, and the annual ploughing contest was one of its first activities. My father won a ploughing contest at one time, using a team of four horses. Ploughing was a precise business, furrows being so deep and so wide. The competition was judged after one morning's work, after which the judges came round to inspect.

*At harvest time we worked all day. In winter it was
7.00am–2.00pm, with breakfast in the field. Then there were
the horses to feed, clean and bed down. If we were working all
day, the horses were changed over. Life expectancy of the shire
horse was not great in those days. A horse over eight was
considered to be old. They could live to twenty-five but not if
they were worked hard. Few reached this age.*

*In 1920 the Central Wages Board awards were made.
Single unemployed people received no benefits. Married
unemployed farm workers got parish relief. Farmers were
opposed to unions, but they began to flourish. The
Agricultural Labourers' Union was formed in 1920.*

*The Friendly Society originated in 1820: the Stagsden
Branch started in 1886, and members met in the Club Room
at the local pub once a month. They were illegal in the first
place, with secret meeting places and secret codes. This was
similar in some ways to the Trade Union. It provided money
for people when sick and death benefit when they died. It cost
1s 9d per month in subscriptions and people drew ten shilling
per week sick pay, reducing to five shillings after six months.
The Provident Dispensary where medical relief was dispensed
(on payment of a small fee), occupied the large stone building
erected in 1887 in St. Peter's Street, which is now the
Probation Office.'*

HORACE WELCH

The Hedger and Ditcher

The most basic function of the hedge was, of course, to
enclose a field and prevent grazing animals from straying,
but it was also regarded by landowners, as an aesthetic
addition to any rural scene, something to give pleasure to the
beholder and a degree of prestige to the land owner. No
formal garden would be complete without its immaculate
hedge, and country lanes and approaches to country
properties were regarded as an appendage to the often
exquisitely cultivated gardens.

It is said that, in Duke Herbrand's time in particular, any approach to Woburn was kept immaculate. Bletchley Railway Station being the main line railway halt for Woburn, a car would be sent to collect visitors from there and approach the estate via Little Brickhill on Watling Street. There were woods on either side of the road as there are today: a long stretch of beech and box hedge fenced the left hand side and was trimmed to perfection straight and level. This was the province of the 'Woods' department for which the head forester was responsible. The amazing thing about it all was that it was cut by a tool called a 'slasher' wielded by hedgers relying on their eye alone to complement their skill with their blade.

On the right hand side of the road any area of perhaps ten yards was planted with flowering shrubs and trees, cherry, laburnum, etc., and rose bushes that gave an appearance of wild woodbine, except the flowers were much larger. Broom and gorse added their contribution. Although they gave the impression of wildness they were carefully cultivated, so much so that a head gardener from Kew met the Duke there to advise on layout, etc. once or twice a year.

All other approaches to the abbey were planted or hedged in similar style but not quite so grand as the Bletchley approach.

'When I left school I worked on the farm. Boys could leave at twelve to work on the land and an order came out that these boys were to 'ave ten shillings a week: men weren't earning much more. Mother said to me to ask if I shouldn't 'ave another shilling or two a week. I was told to go somewhere else and get it, so I went down the road, to Battlesden, to Arthur Syratt the farmer. He gave me a job for another shilling. He knew my grandfather and he said to me "if you make as good a man as your grandfather you'll do well". My grandfather, Levi Creamer, worked on Manor Farm which went with the Battlesden estate. I was still working for

Levi Creamer, Chris's grandfather, at work on the Battlesden Estate.

Mr Syratt when I got married. My wife came from Ridgemont and her father was in the Indian army. He used to drive the Foden steam waggon on the estate – William Walters was his name. He used to fetch coal from Bletchley and so on. He was also Arthur Syratt's 'orsekeeper.

I've used a double plough with four 'orses on the farm. You could do an acre and a quarter a day, or three roods a day with a single plough.

There were many tenant farmers on the estate years ago: now there are about three.

Farmin' was a most interesting job at one time and there were a variety of jobs to be done. Most of the farmers at that time o' the day wan'ed the job done properly. When I built a stack and thatched it I knew it would keep the rain out. They could combust and catch on fire if wet when stacked. It's amazing how much heat grass generates. There was plenty of folks on the farms in them days.

I later worked as a shepherd for Arthur Sturgess at

*Chris Creamer,
hedge laying in
Milton Bryan.*

*Beckerings Manor Farm, which was taken over by the Duke
and run by tenant farmers. I was about twenty-five at that
time.*

*In later years I was mainly a 'edger and ditcher. The finest
bit o' 'edging I ever done on my own was for Arthur Syratt
and that was along the side of an orchard, it was a boundary
'edge. Some thought it was good enough for competition. You
learnt more by watching people work than you did if you
asked questions. You learned as you went. You'd need a good
pair o' gloves, sharp tools and a bill 'ook for your 'edging. You
cleaned the bottom of your 'edge out and left your stumps all*

clean cut so as it didn't 'old the water when it rained. The job needs doing every five or six years. You needed good 'edges to keep the animals in – or out.

Now ya see, when old man Mitchell were Head Forrester, they laid them 'edges round the woods on the estate orf the stump, you know, so's he could stand at one end and look down it and see the stump to one side and the other side where they cut the stakes. All regimental – yeah. Most of the Duke's were regimental – everything 'ad to be regimented, like army fashion. The ditches 'ad to be cleaned and that encourages growth. Now all they want to do is pull the damned 'edges up.

One job that needed doing frequently was the grass "rides". Where they used to ride their 'orses the grass 'ad to be kept short like a tennis court. The over-'anging twigs 'ad to be cut and the turf cambered each side. I've got a photo somewhere.

If you crossed anybody on the estate or the farms, you were out. Toddington was the nearest place to work outside the estate and this was where the rebels apparently went. It was a bloomin' long way to push your furniture on bicycles! You 'ad to keep the peace or you'd be out. As industry moved in – the brickyards, cement works, Vauxhall and so on – people left the land for more money.'

CHRISTOPHER CREAMER

The Ploughboy

'I became ploughboy at thirteen, drilling, harrowing, working with horses every day of the year except on Sundays, and in all weathers. I worked on several farms and was happy on the first farm, but not so the others. It was hard work and poor pay. By the age of fifteen I only earned eleven shillings a week, and had to work six days a week at that. You would work with the horses until 2 o'clock, have lunch, clean out the stables, then feed and bed down the horses. I was driving ploughs the week the first world war finished, and there were *twelve or fourteen horses on the farm then. The horseman and cowman worked seven days a week, feeding and caring for these animals. With the introduction of tractors, the number of horses were reduced, of course.*

The farmer for whom I worked at my first job supplied a field in which we could play cricket, and even loaned me his bat with which to play. This farmer married my sister in the end and so became my brother-in-law. He had around five hundred acres in his early days and remained a farmer all his life, as did his father before him.

I did farm work through necessity, but it was hard work which carried no status and yielded few rewards. You were a common clodhopper, the lowest form of life.'

JOHN 'JACK' THORNE

Working the Fields

'In 1901, due to an Act of Parliament all farms and small holdings were given a number. Before this, most fields were known by their names and I still remember quite a few of them. One of them, almost the farthest from the village, was called Town's Close; other field names were: Green's Close, Babbs, Highbury Hill, Twenty Stitch, Grass Shadings, Further Shadings, Wood Close, Egypt, Hermitage, Clapham Piece, Hoolands, Balls Green, Church Green, The Lynch, Flewton End, Hockley, Home Close, Hollow Field, The Pythle, Gertford, Broad Hedges, Buckets Hole, The Park, Fifteen Acres, Tinkers Acre, Naboths Vinyard, Broad Green, Mill Field, Walkers, Boggins, and Mopbeggar Pond is still to be seen on the outskirts of the field bearing this name.

Thinking back to the year of 1911, the harvest about finished, and the schools still on their summer holidays, the children were all itching to go gleaning, but there was still one shock or stook left in the middle of the field. This was left there as a sign or warning that the field had not been dragged or cleared. During the process of gathering in the harvest, a certain amount which had fallen from the sheaves and would otherwise be wasted, would be gathered up by the horse-drawn rake which was pulled over the field – this being known as dragging or clearing.

As soon as the first field had been cleared, news was spread round the village very quickly and it was a common sight to see forty or fifty women and children gleaning the ears of wheat which had been left in the field. The gleans would stand about the field like dolls, some of them would be tied with string and others would be tied with straws twisted from the glean. Sometimes the parents would come along in the evening to help carry the gleans home.

The gleans would then be threshed, either with a flail or by the threshing machine. I did know of one woman gleaner who gathered enough gleans when threshed to have sufficient wheat to supply the family with flour for the whole year. After the harvest it was a common sight to see two or three teams of horses on a farm ploughing the ground ready for the next crop. On a quiet day one would hear the ploughboy singing, whistling, and cracking his whip as he walked beside the horses pulling the plough whilst the ploughman would be keeping the plough in the furrow. A good team of horses with a single furrow plough would plough at least an acre a day, and to do this it was said that the man and boy had walked a distance of eleven miles.

Usually the farm labourer, if working in the field all day, would, in the winter time, take with him in his workbasket, or "doccy bag", what was known as a Bedfordshire Clanger. This would be boiled suet pudding or roll, inside which was a filling of potatoes, pork and onions. Sometimes the roll, boiled in a cloth, would have a string tied around the middle, and one half would be filled with the savoury ingredients and the other half with jam.'

WALTER 'REG' PARROTT

The Bedfordshire Clanger

The Bedfordshire clanger, a 'sort o' pudden. Suet. Hard as a hog's back' according to H E Bates and Uncle Silas, who claimed to have 'laid her [Miss Tutts] out with a Bedfordshire clanger'.

[Sugar for the Horse. Courtesy the estate of H E Bates and Penguin Books Ltd.]

PASTRY:
4oz plain flour
1 teaspoon baking powder
half teaspoon salt
2oz beef suet
water to mix

FILLING:
5oz meat cut into small pieces
(stewing beef or bacon is best)
small amount diced potato
small amount chopped onion
seasoning to taste
stock/gravy/water
approx. 2 dessert spoonfuls jam
(plum or apricot are good:
choose a firm variety)

Make pastry and shape into oblong. Reserve small portion of pastry and make a bridge along. Spread meat, potato and onion on larger portion; season to taste and moisten with a little gravy or stock. Spread jam on remaining third. Roll up with care; seal edges with water. Lightly flour the clanger; wrap in buttered or greasproof paper and a pudding cloth and secure. Place in boiling water and simmer for approximately 2 hours. Serves 1–2.

Thrashing

'It was usually an exciting time when we heard that the thrashing tackle would be coming to the farm on a certain day – weather permitting. As I have mentioned before, extra hands would be needed probably about a dozen. With the engine, drum and elevator all set in the rickyard, the first job to be done was to remove the thatch from the roof of the stack. The wooden spits or pegs that bound the thatch to the roof would be carefully tied into bundles and stored away in the barn, ready for use the next year.

After breakfast all was ready, and, with steam up, a start was made. Two men would be on the corn stack and two or three on the straw stack. It was interesting to see, as time went on during the day, the cornstack disappeared and the straw stack grew rapidly.

John Campion's uncle, Edward Campion, who farmed at Knotting Green, originally owned this steam engine, which was used for hauling the thrashing machine and for driving it. He gave up farming in 1914. The derelict engine was recently purchased and restored by 'Olverson' of Southampton, who contacted John as the original owner. It is now proudly exhibited at steam rallies around the country. Photo: courtesy Mr John Campion.

Thrashing team from Hookers at Milton Ernest.
Photo: courtesy Mr Reg Parrott.

It was almost a full time job for one man or strong boy to carry water for the thirsty engine, either from the well, pump, or pond, the engine man always insisting on using clean water.

Two men would be busy carrying the chaff and cavings into a barn, as these would be useful by-products. The chaff would be mixed with chopped swedes or mangel-wurzels, oatmeal and linseed cake for feeding to the cows, and the cavings would be used for litter in the pigstys and cowsheds. It would keep two men busy looking after the corn sacks. A good yield would be from fourteen to twenty sacks, each weighing two-and-a-quarter hundredweights being taken off the drum every hour. They were then weighed on a weighing machine and carried into the barn. The sacks could be borrowed from any railway station at the rate of 1d per week. It is now illegal to carry such heavy weights, the maximum being permitted at one hundred and twenty pounds. Short breaks would take place at eleven o'clock and four o'clock, with the lunch break in between. The farmer or his wife would usually bring out the welcome refreshing drinks, which helped to wash away the dust from the men's throats.

When the job was finished, the engine men would pack up the tackle and get ready to move on. If the traction engine was moving some distance by road to the next farm, the farmer would have to provide a flagman to ride in front of the engine, on a bicycle, just in case of meeting a frightened horse. One could often hear the thrashing tackle, or as the old men used to call it "the farmer's fortune teller", jingling along the road, travelling from one farm to another. The description "fortune

The Corn Exchange, George Street, Luton. The Gothic-style building was erected in 1868, on the site of the old Market House and adjacent to the Ames Memorial where formerly the 'stocks' were placed. A busy scene each Monday, when farmers gathered to sample 'seeds' and to discuss prospects of the season.
Photo: Luton and Neighbourhood Illustrated, publisher T G Hobbs.

teller" was derived from the fact that the farmer would not know the success or failure of his crops until after thrashing had taken place, and the actual yield could be seen. Today, with one fell swoop, the modern combine harvester enters the cornfield, and by the time it comes out again, the crop has been cut, thrashed, and the grain carted to the farm to be stored into large silos, there to await the arrival of the miller or corn merchant. This is a far cry from the days of harvesting by hand – by cutting with the sickle, and threshing with the flail.'

WALTER 'REG' PARROTT

Moving Dung

'I think the best job I had was when Mr Roberts came into the stable in the morning to announce that there were two or even three trucks full of dung to be collected from the railway sidings at Shefford. these had to be cleared in forty-eight hours after notification that they were in. After that time a demurrage charge would be made and this had to be avoided at all costs. Two men and myself, with a horse and cart each, set off in convoy. The dung was from the London stables and in it we found dead cats, dogs and even a small dead pig. One of the advantages of going on hard roads was that we were allowed the use of long reins, which were never allowed on the farm: boys had either to walk or ride on the horse's back so to stand in a cart driving with long reins was pure joy.

Arriving at the sidings we had to find the wagons with the name Mr Roberts, Top Farm on the label. Drawing up close would could get two carts alongside one wagon, the other cart drawing up by the second wagon. I followed the advice of the men, or rather did as they did, and by throwing my dung-fork into the wagon and clambering up and over the side of it, I found myself on top of a seven-ton heap of steaming dung. After Bandy had loaded his cart he helped me so all three of us returned at the same time. The carts were fitted with *extensions called dung-boards, enabling us to load extra weight. The top of the load was shaped like a pyramid and we would sit on sacks on top of it. With the reins in my hands and the warmth and steam rising from the dung I was king of the castle. I was quite high up and felt a little unsafe, especially as we had to negotiate a steep incline, but my mare had done it all before. I think I must have had Polly that day. After steadying herself at the top she started her descent slowly but with increasing confidence she leaned back into the breaching, a wide leather strap passed round the haunches, strapped to the saddle and chained to the shafts by means of hooks. Bearing the whole weight of the cart, no less than a ton, she took tiny steps all the way down. She always had three feet planted on the road at any one time. I was rocking back and forward on the top, like riding a camel in the desert. This was the very first time I had brought a loaded cart from the goods-yard. Previously it had been light loads, going in the opposite direction, and this was an exciting new experience for me.'*

STANLEY WHITTEMORE
'Reproduced from an article in the Bedfordshire Magazine,
with the publisher's permission.'

Rabbiting

'During the First World War of 1914–1918, my father was given permission to keep down the vermin on one of the farms of the village. We kept one or two ferrets at home and also a well trained dog. During the winter months most Saturdays would be occupied by us with the catching of rabbits. These would be taken to the farmer who would keep half for himself and give the other half to my father for his labour.

As people were rationed with meat, the rabbit was a much sought after animal, as a good rabbit when skinned and dressed would weight about three pounds. Various methods were used to catch the rabbits, one being by using ferrets to move the rabbits from their burrows. Small nets would be placed over the holes and the ferret would force the rabbit out of the burrow into the net. Another method was catching them by snare, which consisted of a thin wire set in a rabbit run or a rabbit track out in the field. This method of snaring has since been made illegal, also the use of the gin trap.

The other way used, usually by the poacher, was to go out after dark with a very long net of about one hundred yards. This would be run out into the field parallel with the hedge and propped up with hazel pegs at intervals of about eight or ten yards. The wind would have to be blowing in the right direction. When everything was ready, one man would stay with the net, whilst his mate or dog would go into the field and drive the rabbits into the net.

My first experience of going out with the long net was with a gypsy fellow, who after coming out of the army had gone into lodgings with a widow with a small family. He went by the nick-name of Sorrow. I was making my way home one evening in early November when he caught up with me. The pubs had closed and by the strong alcoholic smell, he had had a good drink. It was then that he invited me to accompany him with the long net and I agreed to go. After having supper, we set off into the darkness armed with two nets, one being one hundred yards long and the other fifty yards. When we arrived in the field, a little distance from the hedge where the first "drop" was to be made, it was my job to run out the net. This I did with him following up behind, propping up the net with the thin hazel pegs. When the nets were all set it was my job to go out into the fields and drive the rabbits into the net. After making several drops in different fields, we returned home with a catch of forty-six rabbits.'

WALTER 'REG' PARROTT

COUNTRY PLEASURES

COUNTRY PLEASURES

Introduction

In recent times the Leisure Industry has emerged as a thriving enterprise, catering for those of us fortunate to have time on our hands and money to spend in pursuit of pleasure. However, if you enquire of people born around the turn of the century as to leisure pursuits and hobbies in their earlier years, the typical reply will be 'well, we had little time for

Taking the children for a stroll: a healthy pursuit in town, village or countryside alike: Downs Road, Luton, a smart locality in Edwardian Times.
Photo: Luton and Neighbourhood Illustrated, publisher T G Hobbs.

play and leisure in my time: it was all work and no play, as the saying goes!'. Most people have no recollections of time spent relaxing, or activities designed purely for recreation, and there may be several reasons which explain this. The Protestant work ethic certainly had the effect of highlighting work – rather than pleasure – as having moral value. 'The Devil makes work for idle hands' is an expression still in vogue and this indicates that time spent idling was unacceptable in a Christian society, where work was regarded as an important element in one's life experiences.

In the country in particular, leisure pursuits went hand-in-hand with purposeful activities. Collecting firewood for fuel, helping with the harvest, digging and tending the allotment, picking wild flowers for decorations, gathering wild berries for cooking, collecting acorns for pig food, – all of these activities were intrinsically pleasureable and yet served a useful purpose. Every activity performed by ordinary country folk had a purpose and contributed something to the family and to society. The concept of leisure for its own sake is a more recent phenomenon.

A westerly view from Park Road, south-east of Luton: a popular promenade on summer evenings and at weekends. Making time for a friendly chat.
Luton and Neighbourhood Illustrated, publisher T G Hobbs.

Many of the more simple pleasures and pastimes are still popular

Cycling Club at Sandy in the 1890s. The man at the back is on a penny-farthing, or more correctly, ordinary bicycle. Sandy, on the Great North Road, was a 'Mecca' for cyclists at the time.
Photo: courtesy Mr S Houfe & County Record Office.

Ever-popular football! The Wootton Blue Cross pictured in 1911. In the back row on the left is Mr Harry Sinfield the local taylor, whose home and shop is now the stores and Post Office. Third from left in the same row is Mr Frank Smith, landlord of the Cock Inn, Wootton.

in rural areas. These include country walks, picnics, fairs, cricket, football, tennis, cycling, boating, outdoor bowls, fetes and garden parties, local events, often organised by the 'local', such as Tug-o'-War, street parties to celebrate special occasions, church parades, harvest and other Christian festivals, skating on frozen ponds and rivers (not many years ago the Ouse froze solid in Bedford), school concerts and amateur dramatics, musical entertainment such as the village band or the church and school choir, dances, Bible classes, Scouts.

Dan Albone, Biggleswade inventor, at the wheel. His Ivel Cycle Works mobilised the working man. Cycling for pleasure was a pastime enjoyed by many ordinary people, prior to the advent of the motor car. Ladies' cycles became available from 1887.
Producer of tractors, motorcycles, bicycles and motorcars, among other things, Dan Albone is seen here with his last invention, the Ivel Potato Planter, produced in 1906, the year of his death.
Photo: source unknown.

Every community had its church and vicarage, and it was common for pageants and other events to be held in the grounds on the vicarage, often for the purpose of raising money for charitable causes. The vicar was responsible for the moral well-being of his parishioners, and took a keen interest in them. The vicarage was an informal meeting point for practising Christians and others within the local community. Another venue for country entertainments was the village school.

'Where the old rectory used to be in Church Road [Wootton] near the Memorial, the vicar used to run a club for boys. In the Memorial Institute which was erected after the first world war, there were two large billiard tables there. There were dances and concerts in the school – all local talent. This was village entertainment.'

STANLEY LOVELL

'I belonged to the "Band of Hope" and members of this organisation took a pledge not to drink alcohol. It is connected with the Bunyan Meeting where John Bunyan used to preach, in Mill Street [Bedford], opposite the Fire Station. Many business people belonged to the Bunyan Meeting. We went each Sunday morning to Sunday School when we were children and with the adults in the afternoon. The room where Sunday School met is now marked out for sport. I was surprised to see how it has changed when I went there recently.

I was married at the Bunyan Meeting.'

MABEL HILLYARD

[In the late 19th century the Bunyan Meeting, Bedford, was by far the wealthiest Nonconformist community in Bedfordshire, owning 162 acres of land.]

'*The Mission Hall [Haynes] near my cottage was built in 1907, and I was Caretaker there for twenty-eight years until 1967. On 28 November 1944 a school meals service began at the hall and children were marched up from school for meals. I helped with the cooking for twenty-one years. There is now a church service held there every other Sunday, as part of it is consecrated. The Cubs, Brownies, Guides and WI use it, and there is occasionally a village jumble sale held there.*

The Mission Hall, Haynes.

During the last war there was a whist drive and dance every Saturday night and it was chock-a-block. There was no electricity when we first took it on and the bucket lavatories were emptied at the top of my garden! It was a long while after the second world war before sewage connections were made.

I was confirmed in 1924 at St. Mary's Church, and I've been a choir member since then. I attend choir practice each Thursday.'

BEATRICE MAY WEBB

There were other regular events which provided opportunities for pleasurable pursuits, and obviously those which were associated with the Christian calendar.

The Country Show

Bedfordshire has a long tradition of country shows, held throughout the summer season, from village show to County Show, but all providing wholesome family entertainment and enjoyment. Such shows are a major attraction for country folk in particular, but have also become popular with urbanites curious about or envious of, country life. Country shows promote competition among exhibitors, publicise local enterprise, highlight agricultural and horticultural developments, attract sponsorship and support local causes and charities. They are a major event in the country calendar.

Falconry – an ancient art preserved.
Photo: courtesy the South Beds.
Agricultural Society.

The country show provides something for everyone, and highlights many aspects of traditional and modern country life. One might expect to find falconry displays, dog shows, terrier racing, ferret racing, rural craft demonstrations, Punch and Judy shows, exhibits of livestock, floral art, agricultural and horticultural displays, a bandstand, trade stands, and refreshments which include fresh country produce and home-made cakes.

An important show in this county is the South Beds. County Show which is staged by the South Beds. Agricultural Society, and organised by volunteers. This began as a gymkhana and has grown to become a two-day Show, held at Herne Manor Farm, Toddington, and is

Undoubtedly a prize-winner.

Photos: courtesy The South Beds. Agricultural Society.

The ever-popular equestrian event.

designed to entertain town and country folk alike. This popular and major local event promotes the countryside through fostering an understanding of rural England. Among the many local organisations which it supports, are the Luton and Dunstable Hospital Special Care Baby Unit, Home Farm Trust, Riding for Disabled, Toddington School Special Needs, Woburn Heritage Centre, Appledore Community Support and Luton and Dunstable Hospice.

Among the many attractions at the South Beds. County Show are archery, clay pigeon shooting, equestrian events, livestock including cattle, sheep and goats, a floral arts and horticultural marquee providing competitions in pot plants and cut flowers, floral art, vegetables and soft fruit, cookery, handicrafts, photography, wine, bees and honey and children's classes. In the canine section, 1,500 dogs are entered at the show each year, grouped as working dogs, utility dogs, toy dogs, gundogs, terriers and hounds. Rural crafts displayed include basket work, caning and rushing, straw platting, corn dollies, lace making, smithying and many more. The South Beds. County Show is an impressive achievement, but it illustrates the popularity of the country shows, which have grown in size and esteem over the years.

Of more humble proportions, yet equally as important for those organising, participating, and enjoying it, was the Keysoe Horticultural Society's Annual Show held in Oxford Farm Grounds, Keysoe. This is more typical of early twentieth-century country shows, and was open to entrants from Keysoe, Bolnhurst, Bushmead, Colmworth, Little Staughton and Pertenhall. Exhibits included Plants in Pots, Cut Flowers, Vegetables, Fruit, Butter, Eggs and Honey, Rabbits, Utility Poultry, Needlework, Lace, and Knitting. For 'children attending day school' there were – among others – classes for Best Specimen of Plain Needlework, Best Specimen of Brush Drawing from Nature, Best Hand Writing of Rudyard Kipling's 'If'.

Keysoe Horticultural Society.

Schedule for 1928.

THE NINTH

ANNUAL SHOW

WILL BE HELD ON

MONDAY, AUGUST 6TH, 1928,

IN THE

Oxford Farm Grounds, Keysoe,

(By kind permission of Mr. E. G. Sharman).

—o—

LIST OF OFFICERS, COMMITTEE, RULES, REGULATIONS, COMPETITIONS, &c.

—o—

President : MR. S. NEWELL.

Committee :

MESSRS. E. GEORGE, W. GELL, F. GEORGE, B. HARTOP, J. HULL, G. RUFF, J. RUFF, E. STAPLETON, A. STAPLETON, A. WHITLOCK, A. WILDMAN, J. WOOLSTON.

Representatives from Bolnhurst :

MR. F. STEWARD, MR. H. WHITMORE, SENR.

Representatives from Colmworth and Bushmead :

MR. S. LACK, MR. C. THOMPSON.

Representatives from Little Staughton :

MR. H. HALL, MR. H. RUFF, SENR.

Representatives from Pertenhall :

MR. A. PEDLEY, MR. G. TAYLOR.

Hon. General Secretary : MR. G. R. ROLLS.

Hon. Assistant Secretary : MR. W. WOODWARD.

Hon. Treasurer : MR. E. G. SHARMAN.

Thomas M. Parker, Printer, Kimbolton.

The Keysoe Horticultural Society's Annual Show. Courtesy Mr A J Woodward.

The Keysoe Annual Show was held in the Oxford Farm Grounds at Keysoe 'by kind permission of Mr E G Sharman': in more recent years, his daughter, the late Mrs Gwen Woodward, wrote of the Show:

'The Committee was busy long before the Show Day – in fact, when one show was over they started planning for the next. Preparations really began the week before when Arthur and Elijah Stapleton came to make a start on erecting the tent. First the post holes were dug and then the wood was carried from the farm buildings where it had been stored in the rafters from the previous year. When the skeleton framework was complete it was covered with rick cloths borrowed from the neighbouring farms. On the great day the Committee arrived very early and soon after daylight competitors started bringing their exhibits.

About 11.00am the judges arrived and my mother prepared lunch for them and others who had been working since early morning. I can remember the huge joint of beef Herbert Stanton [see front cover] delivered and also a whole ham. I often thought longingly of those lunches during the war years! The classes which created the most interest – at least for the ladies – were the Table Decorations which took up nearly the whole centre of the tent. One class was for any flowers, one for home grown flowers and foliage and another for anyone who had never before won a prize.

Admission to the field was 1/- at 2.00pm and 6d after 5.00pm. There were sports for the children in the afternoon and for adults in the evening and also a fancy dress parade. There were coconut shies, skittles and ninepins and sometimes hoopla. Other entertainment was provided such as a conjurer. Mr Harold Woodcock catered for teas in a large marquee under the walnut trees. Music was provided by the Kimbolton Silver Band who also played for the dance held in the school in the evening. The villagers provided a sweet stall on the field, as no tradesmen were allowed inside, but some did set up stalls by the roadside – Mr Freddie Mayes,

Mr Caress and Mr George Brown and an ice-cream man. Cars were parked for two or three hundred yards along the road, but as most people arrived by cycle in those days these were stored in the rickyard at 2d at time. One of the highlights every year was "Who Won the Bike?" I cannot quite remember how this was done, but I think that a watch would be wound up, placed in a box which was then sealed, and tickets would be sold which each had a different time on them. The person with the ticket showing the exact time when the watch had stopped would be the winner of the Raleigh cycle. I think that this was so popular that in the latter years two watches were used and two cycles – a Ladies' and Gents' – were the prizes. Two people I remember who were lucky in this draw were Arthur Askew and Harry Pedley.

Fourteen days after the Show we all took our Prize Cards to the school and received our prize money, and that was the end of the Show for another year.'

Article Courtesy Mr A Woodward

A Carnival Procession in Dunstable, to celebrate the George V Silver Jubilee (1910–1935). Photo: courtesy Dunstable Gazette.

'My sister, Phyllis, was a nurse. She never married. We used to show dogs, even before the war. This was when she went into nursing. My mother had a golden retriever at this time and there was a country show at Sandy, a one-day event. We entered her and she took first prize. She went on to win prizes at the Kempston Show. We began breeding dogs, and showed at Northampton, Birmingham, Scotland and other places and took a very good prize at Crufts.'

WILLIAM CONSTANT

'I have often acted as Steward at the Bedford County Show and at the East of England Show at Peterborough.

I do enjoy beagling, which is something I've done for fourteen years. This entails walking across muddy fields, and over other people's land. I call it "licensed trespass" – you can cross private land and see what people are getting up to! The beagle is smaller than the foxhound, around sixteen to eighteen inches, with shorter legs. You set off in pursuit of hares with perhaps as many as thirty or forty people, men and women, young and old. Nine times out of ten the hare gets away.'

JOHN CAMPION

The Local

The Pub, or 'Local' as it was often known, has long been an integral part of village life, together with the church, chapel and school, and has for centuries been an important facet of the village community. As the influence of the Church waned, despite the efforts of the Temperance movement for abstinence, the pubs flourished. During the times of the depression, drinks at the local with other unfortunates, must have provided some comfort and solace for the unemployed.

The pub has provided a valuable service to local communities, in particular, in rural areas. The traditional pub provided a meeting place which could be homely, warm and cosy, a refuge, often with inglenook fireplaces, roaring log fires, oak-beamed walls, horse brasses, ceiling beams hung with mugs and tankards, stone flagged floors, smoke-stained ceilings and walls, smoke-filled rooms, opaque glass partitions, wooden seats or settles, and tucked away in some corner, the piano. Pubs catered for local needs and local customers, and pub names often reflected local interests and trades, for example, 'The Brick Maker's Arms', 'The Angler's Rest', 'The Airman' and 'The Slater's Arms'. Pub architecture reflected local tastes and utilised local materials.

The character of the pub has changed in recent times, with upmarket trappings, reproduction oak furnishings, thick carpeting, serving hatches and salad bars. Now a place for young 'trendies' and for those seeking good food and drink in a traditional setting, this is a far-cry from the pubs our fathers and grandfathers knew.

After the Industrial Revolution, separate bars became popular in pubs, catering for the working classes or for the more middle class client. These bars were usually known as the Public Bar and the Saloon Bar (the 'half-a-crown' side) or the Smoke Room. In practice, the Saloon Bar was more often used by courting couples or women escorted by husbands. These offered somewhat more comfortable surroundings and greater privacy, but drinks in the Saloon Bar were normally priced higher than those in the Public Bar. Country pubs were the preserve of men, male refuges! Women did not frequent pubs alone, and few accompanied their men-folk. Wives grudgingly accepted their partner's drinking habits, but since many men laboured in manual occupations, particularly on the land, a drink at the pub was regarded as a necessary social pastime, affording the opportunity for a few moments of quiet relaxation and enjoyment of the company of other working men, after a hard day's work.

Many pubs had a Club Room which could be hired or used for special occasions. Friendly Societies met in the Club Room, – self-help groups – whereby men paid money into the

Club from wages, and this would be used to supplement income during periods of illness or to cover expenses upon death. Any money left in the 'kitty' at the end of the year would be shared among members. These were referred to as Sick Clubs or Slate Clubs. Payments were known as 'didlums'.

Locals at the village pub enjoyed beer on draught, and food was never available or required other than for a special occasion such as the Dart League match night. Working class people didn't want to buy food at the pub. Women were never encouraged to participate in pub games: they weren't encouraged to visit the pub. This arena was male-dominated, a male preserve, and generally a meeting place for older men, and less for the local youths. Among the most popular games at the local were Dominoes, Crib, Skittles, Shove-ha'penny and Darts.

The smell of stale ale permeated the public house, together with that of nicotine (virtually all men of this generation smoked cigarettes, pipes or cigars, or chewed 'baccy' or took 'snuff'). And as for smells, it was just as well that most pub toilets were external! A quick trip across the yard to a cold, unheated, foul-smelling corrugated-roofed urinal must have tested the tenacity of the most enthusiastic drinker.

Most men had a pub night, and would turn up as regular as clockwork for their usual. Drinks were sometimes taken on credit, referred to as 'on tick' or 'on the slate', and the week's bill settled on payday. The landlord and locals knew when to expect individuals, and if they didn't turn up on time, the landlord would be wondering why.

'We opened from 10.00am to 2.00pm and 6.00pm to 10.00pm (10.30pm in the summer), and on Sundays from 12.00–2.00pm and 7.00pm–10.00pm. At 10.00am Mr Henry Swaffied, who was a big noise locally and ran the County Show, called in and had a half-pint and left. Then his son came and had his half-pint. We always had regulars and you

knew what time they would come and even what they would say when they arrived. At 11.00am the burners came. They worked on top of the kilns, putting coal-dust in to regulate the heat. Now it's done by instruments but in those days it was hand work. They worked in Stewartby but many lived in Ampthill, Maulden and local villages, and they'd call in for a drink as they passed through. It was all beer on draught at that time. If they didn't come you would miss them and wonder where they were. We used to get the village coppers come to the back door for their drink, often about closing time.

We did a lot of business after the A6 murders at Deadman's Cross. The Magistrates Court used to be in the middle of Ampthill, and this case which involved Hanratty, attracted crowds of people. We also increased trade when the Pram Race was held. We were at the pub when it started, and it was run from Chimney Corner to Ampthill. It was in support of the ex-servicemen's charity. Also, there used to be a cinema next to the pub called the "Zoniter" and people came in for a drink after the showing, and that boosted trade too. Other than that, it was all local trade, and always regulars. We had a steady trade all the year round. Flowers owned it when we took over, and then Whitbreads, but my father had it before me, when it was owned by J W Green. My mum and dad were there in the '40s, when the men were demobbed after the second world war, and had their gratuities to spend. That was good for trade.

The pub was very old, with low ceilings downstairs but high ceilings upstairs, and low doorways, so you had to step up into the room, and duck down at the same time, when entering.

When men met over a drink, they never talked about sex in those days, like they do today. It was usually talk about gardening, the allotments, how many bricks they had burnt and how many they had spoilt. Sometimes they'd talk about their families. The big topic was horse-racing: there was a bookies' shop nearly opposite and they did a good trade with

Photographed at the rear of the Crown & Sceptre, Ampthill in the 1960s, Bert Inskip, market garden trader from Maulden, and one of the 'locals': Jimmy Cameron (right), barman at the White Hart (then known as the 'posh pub'); Ted White (left), Landlord of the Crown & Sceptre, and to the rear, Ivor Warren, also a barman at the White Hart. The Penny Farthing was owned by Ted's father, who was the previous Crown & Sceptre Landlord.
Photo: courtesy Mr T White and Echo & Post Ltd., Hemel Hempstead.

the customers. They all came by bike, nearly all our "regulars".

You never saw the wives at the bar. Many of the Maulden wives worked on the land, some took in hat work. On one occasion a local lady came looking for her husband and my wife met her outside the pub. She said she'd looked everywhere and couldn't find him. The wife told her he was in the pub and there was a terrible row. Most wives were understanding or tolerant, but I've known several to come in in a rage, carrying the old man's dinner and slap it on the counter! Most men would only have two or three pints and then go home as sober as they came. At the weekends we would have a sing-song and about enough drink to make them merry.

Then the Wingfield Club was started, after the first world war, for ex-servicemen, and this was a better place for the women, – a better place for a man to take his wife for a drink.

We didn't organise day trips from our pub, although some publicans did. The locals might organise a day out to Newmarket for the horse racing, hire a coach. The darts team perhaps.'

(Mr Ted White, Retired Landlord, The Crown & Sceptre, Ampthill)

Many pubs organised day trips and booked coaches or charabancs for summer outings to the seaside, and families who couldn't afford a holiday away, would go and have a good day out together. Drinks would be loaded aboard for a stop-over, and there'd be a sing-song during the journey, with young children asleep on mum's lap long before the excursion reached home, late at night.

Day Trips and Other Pastimes

'We used to go to whist drives at the school at Felmersham. We'd have chapel outings once a year, to the seaside by charabanc [a motorised, single-decker bus]. I've got a photo of my mother taken at the seaside. They had to take the side of

A charabanc outing from Bedford, 1924.
Photo: courtesy Mr S Houfe and The Bagshawe Collection.

Ivy's mother pictured on the beach at Clacton, enjoying a day-trip in true British style, hat, coat and all. 1935.

*the bus off to get mother in, as she was so big: this was when
we lived at Stevington and I was about seven.*

*We'd go by horse and cart to visit my aunt in Rushden (a
governess cart it was). There was always singing for pleasure
at home, to the gramophone. We learned songs from the
records. There was the church choir, card playing, rag-rug
making: mother made them for the WI to sell for about five
[old] pence a time. We did knitting and needlework. My
grandmother made lace [hobby and occupation]. There was
cycling, walking, and for us children, hoops, whip and top,*

*Totternhoe Knolls near Dunstable, popular with visitors. A local
nature reserve, well-known for its orchids and insect life. The Knolls lie
to the west of Dunstable. Its Woodland walks are as popular as ever,
and the picnic site attracts country lovers throughout the summer.*

*The London and North Western Railway Company arranged cheap
excursions from London to Dunstable on Sundays at 3/- [three
shillings, or 15p] for a half-day, and 4/- Saturday to Monday.*

*Photo: J Field, from 'Dunstable – a Healthy, Bracing Spot in
Bedfordshire', printed by Waterlows in 1905.*

hop scotch and primrosing. My aunt made wine from the primroses and cowslips. We dried them and got six pennies a pint for them! We measured them in a pint pot. There was blackberrying, gleaning, potato picking, animals to care for, eggs to collect. When I was older we played crib, darts and dominoes and skittles at the local pub: we played for drinks. The annual trips to the seaside by charabanc were organised from the pub.'

IVY FLUTE

Franklins' (Coal Merchants of Northampton) country house in Radwell, at Moor End, 1928. The Miniature railway was built for their children, but other local children were also invited to use it. Ivy, second from left, is pictured here with her cousins, on one such occasion.

'We used to do some rum things at times when I was younger. We came to live in a cottage by the school in Keysoe, Rose Cottage. I can remember pluming and throwing plums to the soldiers, climbing trees and sliding down the boughs, playing by the ponds and then running about to get dry. We'd tie a rope around ourselves and go into the pond! We went moorhens nesting, birds nesting. Mother used to cook the eggs we found – lovely eggs. My dad reared Bedlington Terriers. We often played ball games as children, as there was nothing on the roads then. I went

*in a pony and cart to have my tonsils and adenoids out in
Bedford Hospital, – went in the morning and came home in
the afternoon! I was about fourteen then. We'd go to Clacton
on a day trip once a year, and every year we had a holiday at
Hockliffe, or went to Tunbridge Wells in Kent, staying with
relatives. We'd pack up the tin trunks and they went by train,
ahead of us.'*

ESTHER IVY DARRINGTON (née ROLLS)

*As children we played hopscotch, skipping, and things like
that. I was the only girl in the school to have a bicycle at the
age of eight. I was brought up in a good home, and my
education was paid for. Father died when I was two, and my
mother when I was five. I was brought up with my maternal
grandfather and stepgrandmother. I was always told to
speak when I was spoken to, but although strict, they were
good to me. Poor children had rag dolls, but I had a
beautiful doll. We used to go on holiday by train and stayed
at a Guest House. Grandfather was working then, until 1919.
He was a signalman on the railway. His father and great
grandfather were gentlemen farmers. I have never known
want.'*

GRACE LOUISA FREEMAN (née ABRAHAMS)

*'I always wanted to retire to the village, but my husband
feared there would be little for us to do in Wootton. However,
since returning, I find my amusement at the Evergreen CLub
held at the Memorial Hall, and bowls at the Village Hall, and
dancing now and again. there was nothing at all years ago, of
course. Bob Lunnis, a local man who died some years back,
left a lot of money and a bequest for an annual dinner to be
held for elderly people in the village. This is an event which
we thoroughly enjoy. The Lunnis family had a shop at the
bottom of Cause End Road, and owned the house right at the
bottom, where he had his carpenter's workshop.'*

SARAH HILLS

Single Days Spent in the Village

'Before I married, at twenty-five, I went around with a gang of friends, boys and girls. Most are dead now. Our pleasures were walking, exploring woods and fields, and cycling. I was never keen on dancing. I chose to spend my free time in the country. My husband-to-be lived in the village where I first went to teach and that was where I met him. There was a gang of young men: you cannot imagine if you have not known village life, what it was like. Our group of young people always went around together and we gradually paired off. We went to church together – you were expected to attend church – attended concerts: my mother-in-law and father-in-law took part in the village concerts. The school organised some of these events, with the approval of the vicar, as it was a church school.

I hated it when I first came to Maulden. I felt that Bedfordshire people did not accept me for a long time. There were feuds even between villagers, – always animosity. Men often came to blows when girls were courted by "outsiders".'

GLADYS WALLIS

'My wife lived at Bromham before we married. We cycled backwards and forwards to meet during our courtship, sometimes going into Bedford on Saturday evening, and occasionally visiting the cinema. My very first visit to a cinema was at the age of fourteen, when I went to the Picturedrome near the river to see "Adam's Rib". It was usual to go for walks and to visit each other's homes and visit church together. Dancing was considered immoral in my community, and my parents never encouraged me to go dancing.'

HORACE WELCH

Single Days Spent in Bedford

'I met my husband at a dance. Pictures and dancing were the means of entertainment in Bedford then and there were lovely dance halls. You could walk home from a dance at midnight with no fear of being accosted. We paid thre'pence for the Picture Palace. There were dances held at the Corn Exchange, Crofton Rooms, Grafton Rooms and the Drill Hall. They were all popular dance places and they had proper bands. Lew Keays was one I can remember and I can also remember when Fay Compton came down to visit the Corn Exchange and I actually saw her there. It was 2/6d entrance that night, a special promotion, and they had the Paramount Players on. It was normally less than that to get in and in fact we called these dances the "sixpenny hops".

Another thing we used to do when we were young was the half-mile swim from the town bridge to the Boat House. The steamers were kept by the bridge then. I belonged to the Bedford Swimming Club who organised the swim and awarded the Colby Sharpin Cup to the winner. He was a doctor you know.'

MABEL HILLYARD

The river and promenade, Bedford, in Edwardian times. A picturesque scene, still popular throughout the year. Fishing, boating, sculling, the Regatta and Water Festival are among the present-day attractions the river scene offers. Ever popular with strollers and as a picnic area. Swimming in the river is now actively discouraged.

Mayday Celebrations

Mayday celebrations have been held throughout the country since Roman times, when it is said that youths danced on the first day of May (the Calend in Latin), in honour of Flora, goddess of fruits and flowers. In Britain, celebrations often took the form of Morris dancing and the use of the maypole.

In Bedfordshire such celebrations have been held at Ickwell and Elstow for many years, and local schools have played an important part in these events, one in particular, being Elstow School.

Elstow Mayday celebrations were traditionally held on the first Thursday in May, at three and six o'clock in the afternoon. The May Queen would be crowned at three o'clock, after which the dancing commenced. Cardington Weather Station gave a forecast at 11 o'clock on the Thursday and if rain was forecast, the celebrations were cancelled and held the following week. An occasional thunder storm sent crowds scattering: some rushed to the church for cover, some the Moot Hall. Colours drained from the abundance of crêpe paper!

Until 1958 children at Elstow School, aged between five and fifteen, came from the rural areas of Willington, Cople, Cardington, Shortstown, Cotton End, Haynes, Wilstead and Elstow. In 1958 Abbey [Middle] School was opened, and children from eleven years upwards transferred to this school, which meant that numbers were seriously depleted at Elstow School and the celebrations were modified as a result.

Preparations for Mayday began in February, when the May Queen was elected democratically, by the top class of about thirty children. The May Queen's photograph appeared the following Tuesday in the Bedford Record. All children took part, among them up to twenty ribbon holders from the top two classes, so there would be continuity from year to year when the top class left school. It also included sixteen Matrons of Honour, two Train Bearers (a boy and a girl from the youngest class) one Herald (a boy from the second class, the one with the loudest voice), and four Jesters. The remainder were helpers, and these included three strong boys from the top class, to pull the coach.

As preparations commenced, children would go in search of boughs (either ash or willow, which were light to carry), from the side of the brook or from around the fields. They were then stripped of all foliage and cut down so as not be be higher than shoulder height, and sharpened to a point at the end so the bough could be pushed into the ground. All children who did not have a main part in the event carried a bough, and these were decorated with paper roses, made by the children in their own time, or often by their mothers. The roses were made of crêpe paper in the child's chosen colours. Colours were not generally mixed.

There were many gowns and outfits to be prepared for the event:

The May Queen wore a long white dress, often a wedding or confirmation dress, with a train which used to be attached at the shoulders. The crown, which was a shell, a framework, was wired and covered with white and pink buds, and the Queen always carried red roses made of crêpe paper, and wore white shoes.

The Maids of Honour wore white short dresses, with silver-painted ivy leaves for a headdress, and carried boughs with pink almond blossom, also hand-made from crêpe paper, white shoes and socks, and they carried a posy of pink rosebuds.

The Train Bearers were always a boy and a girl. The girl wore a long white frock like a bridesmaid's dress, and the boy wore white trousers, white shirt, school tie, and a buttonhole-type posy.

The Herald wore white trousers, a hunting red jacket and black top hat. The same hat was brought out year after year, and fitted some better than others. It often had a newspaper pushed inside to keep it from falling over the ears and face!

The previous year's May Queen, who crowned the new Queen, wore a colourful dress, often a bridesmaid's dress, in a colour of their choice. As a headdress she wore a circle of flowers. The previous year's May Queen would by this time, have left school, and returned for the occasion, to take part.

Jesters wore red and green outfits, hats with bells.

Electricity for the gramophone came from the Moot Hall, and a Loud Speaker system was used, although this was less than effective on a windy day.

On the day of the festival, the children began dressing after dinner. Those without a job to do just wore their prettiest frocks. The throne and steps went to the village green late morning. As the procession commenced in the afternoon, reporters were on hand, and police held up the traffic. First came the ribbon holders, who were attached to

The procession leaving Elstow School. Pictured in the early 1950s are (left to right and front to back): Alan Fuller, Donald Wildman, Elizabeth Walters, Victoria Lambert, Margaret Norman, Beverley Brown, Patricia Garrett, Joyce Ward, John Hillingsworth, Joan Hartnett, Alan Stanton, Mrs Eveley, Alan Bartram (now a Luton Travel Agent), Terence Farmer, Linda Gilbert.
Photo: courtesy Mrs L Warner (née Gilbert) and Mr A Drake Sadler, Photographer.

Leaving school via the Headmaster's gate, en route for Elstow Village Green. The original Bunyan's cottage can be seen on the left of the picture.
Photo: courtesy Mrs L Warner and Mr N Verby, Photographer.

In control! The Ribbon Holders.
Photo: Courtesy Mrs L Warner and Mr A Drake Sadler, Photographer.

the maypole and they all proceeded in a certain order, assuming their positions as the maypole was erected. The coach followed the maypole. Riding in the coach were the Queen, the Train Bearers, and the Herald. Following the coach, on foot, were the Maids of Honour, and everyone else followed on behind.

Once assembled on the green instructions were given by the chief hailer, the Herald, over the tannoy, 'the Queen commands that the maypole be erected', and this was done. Then the command 'ribbon holders run', and off they went: they all knew who to follow so the ribbons fanned out in the correct manner. Each ribbon had to come down straight, with no crossed ribbons. The ribbon holders didn't do all the ribbon dances: they held the ribbon, which would be handed over to other children for particular dances in between times. Ribbons were multi-coloured.

Queen at Eleven! Crowning of the May Queen, Jennifer Carding, of Elstow Infant School following the opening of the new secondary modern school (Abbey) in Elstow, 1958. A peal of bells signalled the crowning, performed by the former Queen, 15-year-old Janet Cooper of Cople. A telegram of congratulations was received from Her Majesty the Queen.
Photo: courtesy County Record Office and The Express & Times.

The coach went around the arena on a lap of honour after the crowning, then the Queen made her speech, followed by the comments 'The Queen commands that the dancing begin'. Following each dance, a further command would be given by the Herald, working through the programme of events.

The maypole dances included the Barber's Pole, Single Plait (with the dancers weaving in and out), Double Plait (with two dancers weaving), and the Spider's Webb (which was like a huge umbrella, once the weaving was completed). On windy days the ribbons sometimes flew away or were difficult to control! Other dances performed between the maypole and the children seated behind their boughs, dug in to the grass, were Strip the Willow, Celendars Round, and We Won't Go Home 'til Morning. There would be four or six groups dancing at the same time.

There were guests in attendance at Mayday celebrations, seated in the guest enclosure, these normally being the Headmaster, his wife, the May Queen's parents, the vicar, persons from the Education Department, the Mayor, and school governors. All other spectators stood or seated

The Boughs.
Photo: courtesy Mrs L Warner and Mr A Drake Sadler, Photographer.

themselves on the grass. Staff at the school assisted in the organisation throughout the afternoon, and the canteen lady did a lovely tea in the hall for the guests and the May Queen but everyone else ended up outside with an iced lolly!

One year the festivities were televised. A local lady who participated on that occasion, recalls that it was the year of the Oxford and Cambridge Boat Race when the Cambridge boat sank – 1951 possibly.

During the proceedings a basket of white doves was released over the green, and a blanket collection was held for the Red Cross or some other charity, when people tossed money onto the blanket.

Ickwell's celebrations were held on the last Saturday in May on the village green.

Of all the children taking part, the Jesters probably had the most difficult role to perform. They had to sort out any problems and to know every dance so they could fill in if anyone were absent. They otherwise carried hoops and generally acted the fool, like circus clowns.

At the end of the event, the proceedings were drawn to a close by the vicar, who offered a closing prayer. Then the command came over the tannoy, 'Ribbon Holders Mass' and the ribbon holders grouped as before, and lifted out the maypole. The Queen, in her coach, shaped like a narcissi, did a last lap around the green and then led the procession back to the school, in the same order as they came in, but the steps and throne followed behind the maypole. The throne was shaped like a tulip, covered with pink and with one petal coming forward. The steps were always painted green.

The Queen's duties for the following year included such things as opening fetes and other events.

The Statty

A tradition of long-standing was the visit to the village green by the travelling fairground entertainers. These occasions were known to many people variously as the Village Feasts,

At the Village Fair: the 'statty' at Steppingley c. 1900. The steam round-about is set up in the forecourt of the 'French Horn'.
Photo: the late Mr H A Farmer, Ampthill.
Courtesy Mr S Houfe and County Record Office.

the Statty or simply the Fair. Village children thrilled to the excitement of the Fair, with its lights, music, throbbing traction engine emitting oily smells, hissing steam and smoke, cries of the stall-holders, and the excitement of the crowd. The carousel with its gay organ music and colourful horses, the rifle range, hoop-la stalls, coconut shies, cake-walk, haunted house, darts, roll-a-penny, kiddies' rides, helter-skelter. One brief interlude of entertainment for its own sake, to brighten the lives of even the poorest of country-dwellers. Spit rock, toffee apples, candy-floss. Prizes to be won – goldfish, fairings, coconuts, etc. If you had little to spend, you could wander around and gaze in wonderment at the colourful spectacle which often arrived by night and mushroomed into life the following morning.

The 'Fairground People' in the early part of the century

toured the villages with their amusements during the summer, and occupied themselves throughout the long winter months by bundling and selling kindling wood for the fire. Hawkers (usually the women) sold white heather button-holes (considered lucky) and lace, from baskets, door to door. It was considered unlucky not to purchase from a gipsy, and rumour had it that they could even put a curse on you! One wonders who could possibly have perpetuated such

A typical Showman's Living Wagon (the Burton), built in the latter part of the 19th century. this wagon was originally horse-drawn, on wooden wheels. It was converted to rubber tyres in the 1930s, when the 'fair people' obtained a Commer lorry for towing.

This fine example of a Showman's Wagon was acquired in the 1980s by Mr Harry Gilbert, a carpenter, who restored it in his retirement. He rebuilt all the furniture as original, with bow fronted drawers, china cabinet and seats which double as storage lockers. The wagon still contains the original stove.

Photo: courtesy Mrs L Warner.

a rumour! Other services offered by the travellers were horse-dealing, sharpening knives, honing tools, sharpening lawnmowers, and the mending of pots and pans by 'Diddicoys'.

The 'gipsy' travellers toured the countryside in horsedrawn wagons. These compact traditional caravan homes contained fitted furniture, often of highly polished wood, and a wood-burning stove for heating and cooking. Looking at the comparative luxury of the present-day showmen's trailers, it is hard to believe that whole families once occupied these wagons. Delightful as they are, accommodation must have been awfully cramped.

The street Fairs also occupied the main street in some towns, when roads would be blocked off for the day, and traffic diverted.

Boxing booths were another way of making money, by pitting one's skills against those of the prize-fighters. Bare-fisted fights too, in earlier times.

After the Fair left the village green, local children would scour the grass at the scene of the shooting gallery, collecting up the shells, or spent cartridges, which could be placed between the fingers and used to create a whistle.

CONTRIBUTORS

WINIFRED LOUISA ALLAN (NÉE HODBY)

Winnie was born at Knotting Green on 8 January 1919. Her father and his father were also born there, in a tied cottage near the church. Her father spent all his working life on Green Farm, owned by Mr Pike. There were no privately owned properties in the village at that time. Of the six children born to Winnie's parents, one died at the age of twelve with appendicitis.

Winnie's family have always been active church members. Her grandfather was an organist and her father too, both self-taught. One vicar (Rev. Wiggins) looked after two parishes then, Knotting and Souldrop. Most village people were church-goers and at harvest festival and the Knotting Feast the church would be packed to capacity.

Winnie met her husband in Bedford in 1938. He was in the Airforce training at Cardington, but he came from Scotland. He was posted to Mildenhall but they kept in touch and were married on New Year's Eve, 1941. As a time-serving airman, he saw action in the Second World War, and was invalided out in 1944.

GWENDOLINE ELSIE BROWN (NÉE JEFFRIES)

Gwen was born in Clapham on 16 June 1908. Her father was a gardener and gravedigger and for ten years of his life he worked solely as a gravedigger at Bedford Cemetery. Gwen's parents had twelve children, of whom nine survived. Four of her brothers were in the first world war.

Gwen met her husband whilst in service at Sharnbrook, and married at the age of twenty. They had seven children. He was a farm worker having worked for some years at Samuel Whitbread's farm near Shefford, and also at Hill Farm, Chellington, but ill health forced him to leave the farm and he then got a job with the Ministry at Twinwoods (from where Glen Miller took off on his last fated flight).

Gwen's husband died in 1968.

FREDERICK BURRAWAY

Fred, one of seven children, was born in 1905 in a cottage in Cause End Road, Wootton, which has since been demolished. His father worked as a Setter for the London Brick Company, then known as Forders Ltd. Fred has lived all his life in the village and has many memories of Wootton and its people, since his early days.

After a two-year courtship, Fred married his wife at the age of twenty-two and took a cottage near the bakehouse where he worked all his life. He has very happy memories of a lifetime spent in the employ of the Juffs family, local bakers, and maintains that given the opportunity he would love to do it all over again.

JOHN ALFRED CAMPION

John was born on 15 October 1907 at Manor Farm, Knotting. His father was a local man and a farmer: his mother lived in Peterborough before her marriage, but had relatives in Sharnbrook and so was no stranger to this area. They had six children, two boys and four girls.

Farming has always been John's main interest. There was a time when he could have started his own farm, but he chose to spend much of his time caring for his invalid sister, a one-time pupil at Bedford High School. He established an enterprise as an agricultural haulier. The business did well and there was always work to be had. He retired 14 years ago. He believes he made as much money with his lorries as many of the farmers did farming their land.

WILLIAM CONSTANT

Bill's father was born in Bedfordshire, but Bill was born on 29 July 1916 at Hessett, near Bury St. Edmunds, Suffolk, his mother being a Suffolk woman. There were three children in the family, two boys and one girl, but Bill's brother, the last-born of the children, died of meningitis when he was four or five. Bill was nearly five when his parents came to live in Renhold, Bedfordshire, where he remained.

EDITH IRENE ELIZABETH CORNWELL (NÉE CROWSLEY)

Edith was born in Dudley Street, Bedford, on 16 February, 1910. Her parents later moved to Bower Street, near the embankment. She has always been known as 'Irene'.

Irene's husband was related to Jack Cornwell VC, who was in the Royal Navy. She and her husband had six children, and she now has sixteen grandchildren and eleven great grandchildren. She has been widowed for twenty-eight years, enjoyed her married life but is now quietly contented and has never wanted to re-marry: thinks she is old-fashioned!

CHRISTOPHER JOHN CREAMER

Chris was born on 14 December 1903 at Church End, Milton Bryan. His father was a woodman/forester on the Woburn estate. Their home was a charity cottage, belonging to the Milton Bryan Charity. Chris's grandfather, Levi Creamer, worked on Manor Farm, which was part of the Battlesden estate. His mother played the organ at the local church from the time she was nine years old, and her mother – Grandmother Clark – who had always lived in Milton Bryan, died at the age of 97.

Chris officially retired at 65, but received no pension, and has worked since then for a local farmer, hedging and ditching, and helping with the cows.

JIMMY HENRY EDMUNDS

Jimmy was born in Buckinghamshire in 1909, but lived for many years in Great Staughton, near the Bedfordshire/ Cambridgeshire border. He was associated with Bedfordshire in a business capacity, having, among other things, been co-director with Richard Shuttleworth in an advertising venture, the works of which were situated at Old Warden, and having at one time acquired a corn merchanting enterprise in Biggleswade.

Jimmy was a pilot: his first flight was with Richard Shuttleworth in 1931, and this initiation aroused his life-long enthusiasm for flight.

ELSIE ROSE ENGLAND

Elsie was born on 1 July 1905 at 44 High Street South, Dunstable. The property – her parents' home and bakery – was on the corner of High Street South and Britain Street, and the house is now occupied by a firm of accountants.

In her younger days, Elsie worked for a Dunstable firm of herbalists known as Flemons and later called Flemons and Marchant. They employed men to collect dandelion roots, comfry leaves, foxgloves and so on, which were sold to wholesalers for drug houses. They also made their own herbal medicine.

Dunstable was a relatively small place in Elsie's youth, and everybody knew everybody else.

IVY FLUTE (NÉE LAWSON)

Ivy was born on 16 February 1916 at Radwell, a hamlet near Felmersham. Her father was the local rag-and-bone merchant, known as 'Raggy Lawson'.

Ivy's father collapsed and died after a trip to London, in 1950, aged 72. Ivy inherited enough money to send her son to Bedford Modern School and he went on to university and is now a teacher. She remembers her father with admiration and affection.

FREDERICK JAMES FROSSELL

Fred was born at Wood Farm, Wootton Green, on 18 May 1909. The farm belonged to Sir Phillip Payne, and Fred's father was a tenant-farmer there for sixteen years. They later moved to Houghton Conquest where they farmed for three years, until his father found a farm he wanted to buy. They then moved to Wick End Farm in Stagsden, and they have remained in Stagsden for the past sixty-six years.

Twelve years after moving to Stagsden, Fred Married. His wife was from Sherrington, Bucks., and she too was from a farming family. When the Bunyan Farm came up for letting, they took it on, and were eventually able to buy it.

MARJORIE GLENFORD (NÉE BRISTOW)

Marjorie was born on 23 June 1908 at Bottesford which is near Grantham in Lincolnshire. Her father, who worked as a railway carrier, died when she was two. Her mother worked as a cook at various country houses, and Marjorie accompanied her, living-in wherever possible, or alternatively, living with mother's relatives.

Marjorie went into service at the age of fourteen, and spent many years working at

Dame Alice School House, and now lives in a Harpur Trust property in Bedford.

HILDA HAYDEN

Hilda was born in St. Cuthbert, Bedford, on Boxing Day of 1894, and was the last of eleven children. Her father had his own decorating business, and she thinks the family were comfortably-off. The large house in Newnham Street where she grew up, had four bedrooms with two large reception rooms downstairs and a lobby.

During Hilda's courting days she and her sisters were only allowed to take boyfriends home when they had decided if they 'wanted them'. One of her friends became pregnant, and she and her sisters Alice and Connie were told quite bluntly that if anything like that happened to them, father would not have them in the house. She was twenty-nine when she married, but she was a good girl!

SARAH ANN HILLS (NÉE LOWE)

Sarah was born on 3 October 1900 in Cause End Road, Wootton, next door to the shop and the Star Public House. This property has since been demolished. Her grand-mother's home was one of the four Yeoman's Cottages at Chennell's Farm, then owned by Mr Frossell, and it was from there that her mother moved to Cause End Road to live following her marriage. When Sarah was a year old her parents moved to Keeley, Wootton. Both parents were from Wootton, and father was a thatcher by trade. Sarah was only three years old when he died of pneumonia, leaving her mother to raise four children, Sarah being the youngest.

MABEL DORIS HILLYARD (NÉE STANTON)

Mabel was born on 12 December 1913 in Priory Street, Bedford. She had one brother. Her father, Walter Stanton, was a blacksmith. He traded in Commercial Road, where the Council works were. He was actually employed by the Corporation and did all the ironwork for Bedford, all the fancy gates. He was in the army during the First World War and during this time her mother often went out scrubbing floors. He suffered from dysentry whilst in the forces, and his weight reduced to six stone at one time, but he survived the war and returned to his smithy, where he worked for forty-eight years in all.

STANLEY GEORGE LOVELL

Stan was born on 9 March 1909 in Hall End, Wootton. He was one of three children, and his father was a general labourer – a bricklayer's labourer – who worked at the brickworks and for Samuel Foster, the builders in Kempston, where Bushbys are now situated. He also worked for Mr Lunnis, the builder at 'Tags End' which is now called Cause End Road. After leaving school at fourteen, Stan worked at the local brickworks for many years.

Stan was in the St. John's Ambulance Brigade for twenty-five years, at Stewartby and then at Kempston, and only left the Brigade in 1954, when he was diagnosed as having a brain tumour. He received medical training in Sidmouth, Devon and was a male nurse with the RAF at Weeton near Blackpool and then at North Allerton, until he was demobbed. He helped to set it up, in North Allerton, and was there when the first patient arrived. It was like a general hospital for the Air Force. He chose this career course with the RAF because of his experience in the St. John's Ambulance Brigade.

WALTER REGINALD PARROTT

Walter, who has always been known as Reg, was born on 28 January 1901 in a stone and thatched cottage in the village of Milton Ernest.

Reg married in 1927 and set up home in Thurleigh. In 1959 he and his wife acquired a sixteen acre smallholding in Keysoe and planned to grow wheat crops and to use the straw for thatching. Despite the untimely death of his wife in 1963 at the age of 57, he carried on, but after retirement, returned to live in Milton Ernest in a little cottage overlooking the park where he had spent many happy hours in his younger days watching cricket. 'Living by myself was not my way of life, being one of a large family and a family man myself' (Reg was one of eleven children, and he and his wife had four children).

Subsequently Reg re-married, his new wife having been a neighbour and friend of long-standing. They lived in a stone and thatched cottage in Thurleigh Road, Milton Ernest, similar in many respects to the cottage in which Reg was born. From his cottage home he could see the church to the left, and on the right, on Church Green, the school, both of which he attended in his young days.

EYVOR SIBYL PELHAM REID (NÉE DOYNE-DITMAS)

Eyvor was born in India on 11 February 1908, whilst her father, a Major in the Royal Field Artillery, was serving in India. Her maternal grandfather, Sir Phillip Monoux Payne, farmed at Bourne End near Wootton and Eyvor's parents returned to Wootton after the first World War. Her family have been associated with this part of the county for several centuries. In the chancel of Wootton church there are many monuments to the Monoux family, the oldest being a marble monument to Sir Humphrey Monoux and dated 1680.

CONSTANCE MARIE ROBINSON (NÉE SAUNDERS)

Connie was born at 21 Bedford Road, Wootton, on Christmas Day in 1909, which is why she was given the name 'Marie'. She was one of eight children, and her parents had a smallholding at their Bedford Road home.

Connie became a teacher, and her first permanent teaching post was a Wootton Primary School, where she herself had once been a pupil.

EVELINE STANTON

Eveline was born on 10 February 1897 in Colmworth village. There were eight children in the family, five boys and three girls. She had more illness than any of the other children, and yet outlived them all.

After a prolonged illness whilst in her teens, Eveline took up poultry farming – her doctor's suggestion. She would have preferred nursing, but felt she hadn't sufficient strength to cope with the demands of nursing.

SIDNEY ERNEST SUMMERLIN

Sid was born on 10 July 1902 in Stagsden, in a thatched cottage which stood opposite Stagsden church, and was known as the Old Vicarage. There were five children in the family, and his father was a farm worker.

Sid left school and started casual work on the farm until a full-time job came up. Things were very slack at the time. He has continued to work on the farm throughout his working life. Even after retirement at the age of sixty-seven, he worked when the opportunity presented itself. Sid remained a bachelor.

ARTHUR 'LOL' LAWRENCE THEW

'Lol', as he was always known, was born on 31 October 1903 in the end one of three cottages in Harrold High Street, which stood opposite the present garage. There were three children in the family, and his father worked in the leather trade. His grandfather was a shepherd.

After leaving school at 13, Lol wanted to join the airforce, which he could not do until the age of fifteen. He did get as far as London in an attempt to join up, but failed because of his poor eyesight. He also wanted to go to Australia, but could not because his mother would not consent. He subsequently joined his father in the leather industry.

ERIC THORNE

Eric was born on 9 January 1896 in Woburn and was the third child of five. His father owned a butcher's shop in High Street North, Dunstable, at one time, and was always connected with farming and animals.

In 1921 Eric and his brother Cyril sailed to Australia. It was a very hard life and they had to do odd jobs to earn a living. They slept rough many times, not having sufficient money to pay for lodgings. At one time Eric rode a horse in a race and also entered the boxing ring as a contestant, to make money. Cyril met a girl and settled down, but although Eric was not afraid of hard work, he gave up and came home after two years. A year later he married Maude Durante of Houghton Road and settled down in Markyate where their son Frank was born. In 1930 he bought a piece of land in Beale Street from his father and had a house built, in which he lived until his death in 1985.

JOHN 'JACK' CLIFFORD THORNE

Jack, as he has always been known, was born on 2 April 1907 in Ilford, Essex. His father, a monumental mason, was killed in a road accident involving horses, whilst cycling to work. The fourth child in the family was born shortly after the death of her father, and Jack's mother then returned to live near her parents at Cross End, Thurleigh.

Jack, who regards himself as being self-educated, started work on the farm, and went on to do nursery gardening, and then became a gardening chauffeur, which he describes as the best job he ever had. His employers were wealthy people but very nice people who treated him as a 'human being'. He farmed out of necessity, but points out that farming at that time was poorly paid, and carried low status.

GLADYS LILLIAN WALLIS (NÉE FROST)

Gladys was born on 28 August 1904 in Bassingbourne, Cambridgeshire, which is near Royston. There were seven children in the family, of whom six survived, and her father was a police constable. Gladys's maternal grandfather was a blacksmith by trade, but her grandparents also had a small market garden. They lived in Soham in the Fens, between Ely and Cambridge.

Gladys's parents moved around as her father was posted in different places, but she started school in Bassingbourne and 'loved every minute of it'. She went on to become a teacher herself. She married at twenty-five, and met her husband in the village where she first went to teach. He had just come out of the army when she first knew him and after their marriage, they set up home in Maulden, where she has lived since 1929.

BEATRICE MAY WEBB (NÉE JEFFORD)

May, as she has always been known, was born in Hounslow, Middlesex, on 28 July 1906. Her father was Haynes born, and this is where all of his family lived. At the time May was born, he was working as a builder's labourer – a yardman – in Chiswick, and when he was drafted into the army in 1914, her mother moved back to Haynes to be near his family. May's mother was born in Wiltshire, but had been in service in Hounslow before their marriage.

May's father was killed in action on 4 November 1918, a few days before the armistice was signed.

May's husband's family came from near Biggleswade, where his father was a smallholder. He and his parents moved to May's present cottage home in 1919, and they married in 1933. Her mother-in-law was an independent lady who worked on the land and continued to do so until she was in her seventies, at which time she qualified for a pension. May's husband was a farm worker all his life.

HERBERT WELCH

Herbert was born at Stagsden West End, which is about two miles from Stagsden, in July 1914. He was the youngest of eleven children and his father was a horsekeeper who worked for Mr Howkins at West End Farm.

After working for several years on the farm, Herbert left to work on the railway. He was a ganger for five years, but eventually returned to the farm, and rented a tied cottage near Turvey Grove Farm, which is now a built-up area. Ill-health forced him to retire early, and for the last ten years of his working life he was employed at Bromham Hospital.

HORACE GEORGE WELCH

Horace was born in Stagsden West End on 25 October 1907, in his father's small tied cottage. His father was a horse keeper to a local farmer. There were eleven children in the family, eight of whom were born in this cottage. Horace eventually took over his father's cottage, and four of his own children were born there. His mother died aged eighty-seven, and his father at eighty.

When Horace retired from farming, he applied for a Council house and was eventually housed at Wood End, Kempston.

OLIVER WELLS

Oliver, youngest of nine children, was born at Felmersham Grange, Felmersham, on 10 March 1922. The Wells family are well-known for their business interests, being based in Bedford. Oliver maintains that there was never any pressure on him to join the family business – Charles Wells Ltd. – founded by his grandfather in 1876. Ever since his inaugural flight in a DH Moth at the age of ten, his main ambition was to fly. Having left Uppingham at the age of eighteen, he joined the Royal Air Force and gained great satisfaction from being able to fly. Oliver left the Forces in 1956, shortly before the death of his father. Following his father's death he was obliged to help in the business.

Wing Commander Wells was awarded an OBE in 1992 for services to the community in Bedfordshire.

FREDERICK WALLACE WILDMAN

Fred was born on 27 August 1893 at 1 Cross End, Thurleigh. He was the eldest of seven children and was born in the house in which his grandmother was born and where his parents set up home when they married. Fred's father was a carpenter, wheelwright and undertaker. Fred worked for his father before leaving school, and after leaving school at twelve. In later life he was a very energetic member of his community – in particular within the Church, the Cricket Club, in fund-raising and so on.

Fred lived an active and long life, and enjoyed good health. At the age of ninety-four he was breaking bricks to lay a new driveway!

Index to Locations

Ampthill, 8, 73, 76, 148, 149, 164
Ashridge, 44

Barford, 105
Barton, 111
Bassingbourne, Cambs., 179
Battlesden, 72, 118, 119, 171
Beaconsfield, Bucks., 53
Bedford, 8, 21, 31, 32, 43, 53,
  54, 59, 63, 73, 74, 76, 78, 80,
  88, 90, 96, 99, 104, 109, 110,
  115, 136, 137, 151, 155, 156,
  169, 171, 174, 175, 176
Biddenham, 98, 99, 110, 156
Biggleswade, 136, 172, 180,
  184, 186
Bishops Stortford, Herts., 90
Bletchley, Bucks., 117, 118, 119
Bletsoe, 81
Blunham, 50
Bolnhurst, 28, 141
Box End, Kempston, 59
Bourne End, Nr. Wootton, 50,
  53, 58, 176
Bromham, 7, 8, 58, 75, 115, 155
Bury End, Nr. Stagsden, 156,
Bushmead, 141
Cardington, 10, 73, 157, 169
Chellington, 169
Clapham, 32, 33, 59, 169
Colmworth, 141, 177
Cople, 161
Cotton End, 157

Deadman's Cross, 148

Dunstable, 8, 16, 38, 39, 41, 43,
  44, 47, 76, 144, 152, 172, 178

Elstow, 40, 100, 106, 107, 157,
  159, 160, 161
Ely, Cambs., 179
Emberton, Bucks., 57

Felmersham, 32, 33, 73, 150,
  173, 181

Goldington, 65
Great Linford, Bucks., 51
Great Staughton, 172

Harrold, 40, 178
Haynes, 84, 138, 157, 180
Hockliffe, 154
Houghton Conquest, 98, 173,

Ickwell, 157, 163

Keeley, 174
Kempston, 56, 58, 73, 99, 100,
  101, 115, 145, 175
Kempston Bury, 99
Keysoe, 8, 141, 142, 153, 176
Knotting, 37, 125, 169, 170

Lathbury Park, Newport
  Pagnell, Bucks., 66, 67
Little Brickhill, Bucks., 118
Little Staughton, 107, 141
Luton, 21, 23, 43, 61, 71, 127,
  133, 134, 159

Markyate, 178
Maulden, 18, 19, 21, 22, 148, 149, 150, 155, 179
Melchbourne, 32, 34
Meppersham, 107
Milton Bryan, 120, 171
Milton Ernest, 8, 28, 32, 34, 37, 126, 172, 176
Moggerhanger, 8, 29

Newport Pagnell, Bucks., 51, 66
Newton Blossomville, 101, 102
Northampton, 81, 145, 153

Oakley, 32, 54
Odell, 73
Old Warden, 64, 65, 66, 67, , 69, 73, 172

Pavenham, 73
Pertenhall, 8, 23, 141
Peterborough, Cambs., 145, 170

Radwell, 10, 153, 174
Ravensden, 28
Renhold, 35, 170
Ridgemont, 16, 119
Riseley, 8
Royston, Herts., 179
Rushden, Northants., 152

St. Cuthberts, (Bedford), 54, 174
St. Neots, Cambs., 105
Salford, near Cranfield, 99
Sandy, 135, 145
Sharnbrook, 8, 61, 62, 169, 170

Shefford, 128, 169
Sherrington, Bucks., 67, 101, 173
Shortstown, 157
Silsoe, 54
Souldrop, 37, 169
Southill, 73
Stagsden, 31, 32, 36, 98, 100, 101, 104, 112, 113, 114, 115, 117, 173, 177, 180, 181
Steppingley, 164
Stevington, 152
Stewartby, 109, 148, 179

Tempsford, 50
Thurleigh, 23, 28, 41, 42, 82, 176, 179, 182
Toddington, 121, 139, 141
Totternhoe, 152
Turvey, 61, 110, 180
Twinwoods, 169

Whaddon, Bucks., 54
Willington, 157
Wilstead, 157
Woburn, 34, 71, 72, 118, 141, 171, 172, 178
Wood End, Kempston, 110, 181
Wood End, Wootton, 57, 58, 99
Wootton, 22, 27, 29, 30, 39, 50, 52, 56, 57, 58, 60, 95, 103, 135, 137, 154, 170, 174, 175, 176, 177
Wootton Green, 58, 98, 99, 173

Books Published by THE BOOK CASTLE

JOURNEYS INTO HERTFORDSHIRE: Anthony Mackay.
Foreword by The Marquess of Salisbury, Hatfield House. Nearly 200 superbly detailed ink drawings depict the towns, buildings and landscape of this still predominantly rural county.

JOURNEYS INTO BEDFORDSHIRE: Anthony Mackay.
Foreword by The Marquess of Tavistock, Woburn Abbey. A lavish book of over 150 evocative ink drawings.

ARCHAEOLOGY OF THE CHILTERNS: edited by Robin Holgate.
The latest research by authoritative experts throughout the area.

NORTH CHILTERNS CAMERA, 1863–1954: From the Thurston Collection in Luton Museum: edited by Stephen Bunker.
Rural landscapes, town views, studio pictures and unique royal portraits by the area's leading early photographer.

LEAFING THROUGH LITERATURE: Writers' Lives in Hertfordshire and Bedfordshire: David Carroll.
Illustrated short biographies of many famous authors and their connections with these counties.

THROUGH VISITORS' EYES: A Bedfordshire Anthology:
edited by Simon Houfe.
Impressions of the county by famous visitors over the last four centuries, thematically arranged and illustrated with line drawings.

THE HILL OF THE MARTYR: An Architectural History of St. Albans Abbey: Eileen Roberts.
Scholarly and readable chronological narrative history of Hertfordshire and Bedfordshire's famous cathedral. Fully illustrated with photographs and plans.

LOCAL WALKS: South Bedfordshire and North Chilterns:
Vaughan Basham. Twenty-seven thematic circular walks.

LOCAL WALKS: North and Mid-Bedfordshire:
Vaughan Basham. Twenty-five thematic circular walks.

CHILTERN WALKS: Hertfordshire, Bedfordshire and North Buckinghamshire: Nick Moon.
Part of the trilogy of circular walks, in association with the Chiltern Society. Each volume contains thirty circular walks.

CHILTERN WALKS: Buckinghamshire: Nick Moon.

CHILTERN WALKS: Oxfordshire and West Buckinghamshire:
Nick Moon.

OXFORDSHIRE WALKS: Oxford, the Cotswolds and the Cherwell Valley: Nick Moon.
One of two volumes planned to complement Chiltern Walks: Oxfordshire and complete coverage of the county, in association with the Oxford Fieldpaths Society.

FOLK: Characters and Events in the History of Bedfordshire and Northamptonshire: Vivienne Evans.
Anthology about people of yesteryear – arranged alphabetically by village or town.

LEGACIES: Tales and Legends of Luton and the North Chilterns:
Vic Lea. Twenty-five mysteries and stories based on fact, including Luton Town Football Club. Many photographs.

ECHOES: Tales And Legends of Bedfordshire and Hertfordshire
Vic Lea. Thirty, compulsively retold historical incidents.

ECCENTRICS and VILLAINS, HAUNTINGS and HEROES.
Tales from Four Shires: Northants., Beds., Bucks. and Herts.:
John Houghton. True incidents and curious events covering one thousand years.

THE RAILWAY AGE IN BEDFORDSHIRE: Fred Cockman.
Classic, illustrated account of early railway history.

BEDFORDSHIRE'S YESTERYEARS Vol. 1: The Family,
Childhood and Schooldays: Brenda Fraser-Newstead.
Unusual early 20th century reminiscences, with private photographs.

BEDFORDSHIRE'S YESTERYEARS Vol 2: The Rural Scene:
Brenda Fraser-Newstead.
Vivid first-hand accounts of country life 2 or 3 generations ago.

WHIPSNADE WILD ANIMAL PARK: 'MY AFRICA': Lucy Pendar.
Foreword by Andrew Forbes. Introduction by Gerald Durrell. Inside story of sixty years of the Park's animals and people – full of anecdotes, photographs and drawings.

FARM OF MY CHILDHOOD, 1925–1947: Mary Roberts.
An almost vanished lifestyle on a remote farm near Flitwick.

DUNSTABLE WITH THE PRIORY, 1100–1550: Vivienne Evans.
Dramatic growth of Henry I's important new town around a major crossroads.

DUNSTABLE DECADE: THE EIGHTIES: – A Collection of
Photographs: Pat Lovering.
A souvenir book of nearly 300 pictures of people and events in the 1980s.

DUNSTABLE IN DETAIL: Nigel Benson.
A hundred of the town's buildings and features, plus town trail map.

OLD DUNSTABLE: Bill Twaddle.
A new edition of this collection of early photographs.

BOURNE AND BRED: A Dunstable Boyhood Between the Wars:
Colin Bourne. An elegantly written, well-illustrated book capturing the spirit of the town over fifty years ago.

ROYAL HOUGHTON: Pat Lovering.
Illustrated history of Houghton Regis from the earliest times to the present.

THE CHANGING FACE OF LUTON: An Illustrated History:
Stephen Bunker, Robin Holgate and Marian Nichols.
Luton's development from earliest times to the present busy
industrial town. Illustrated in colour and monochrome. The three
authors from Luton Museum are all experts in local history,
archaeology, crafts and social history.

**THE MEN WHO WORE STRAW HELMETS: Policing Luton,
1840–1974:** Tom Madigan.
Meticulously chronicled history; dozens of rare photographs; author
served Luton Police for nearly fifty years.

BETWEEN THE HILLS: The Story of Lilley, a Chiltern Village:
Roy Pinnock.
A priceless piece of our heritage – the rural beauty remains but the
customs and way of life described here have largely disappeared.

EVA'S STORY: Chesham Since the Turn of the Century: Eva Rance
The ever-changing twentieth-century, especially the early years at her
parents' general stores, Tebby's, in the High Street.

**THE TALL HITCHIN SERGEANT: A Victorian Crime Novel based
on fact:** Edgar Newman.
Mixes real police officers and authentic background with an exciting
storyline.

COUNTRY AIR: SUMMER and AUTUMN: Ron Wilson.
The Radio Northampton presenter looks month by month at the
countryside's wildlife, customs and lore.

COUNTRY AIR: WINTER and SPRING: Ron Wilson.
This companion volume completes the year in the countryside.

Specially for Children

VILLA BELOW THE KNOLLS: A Story of Roman Britain:
Michael Dundrow. An exciting adventure for young John in
Totternhoe and Dunstable two thousand years ago.

ADVENTURE ON THE KNOLLS: A Story of Iron Age Britain:
Michael Dundrow. Excitement on Totternhoe Knolls as ten-year-old
John finds himself back in those dangerous times, confronting Julius
Caesar and his army.

THE RAVENS: One Boy Against the Might of Rome: James Dyer.
On the Barton Hills and in the south-each of England as the men of
the great fort of Ravensburgh (near Hexton) confront the invaders.

Further titles are in preparation.

All the above are available via any bookshop, or from the
publisher and bookseller

THE BOOK CASTLE
12 Church Street, Dunstable, Bedfordshire, LU5 4RU
Tel: (0582) 605670